IS MEDIA
VIOLENCE
A PROBLEM?

Other Books in the At Issue Series:

Affirmative Action
Animal Experimentation
Anorexia
Anti-Semitism
Biological and Chemical Weapons
Child Labor and Sweatshops
Child Sexual Abuse
Cloning
Creationism vs. Evolution
Date Rape
Does Capital Punishment Deter Crime?
Drugs and Sports
The Ethics of Abortion
The Ethics of Euthanasia
The Ethics of Genetic Engineering
The Ethics of Human Cloning
Ethnic Conflict
Food Safety
The Future of the Internet
Gay Marriage
Guns and Crime
Heroin
How Should Prisons Treat Inmates?
Immigration Policy
Interracial Relationships
Legalizing Drugs
Marijuana
The Media and Politics
Nuclear and Toxic Waste
Nuclear Security
Physician-Assisted Suicide
Rain Forests
Rape on Campus
Satanism
School Shootings
Sex Education
Sexually Transmitted Diseases
Single-Parent Families
Smoking
The Spread of AIDS
Teen Sex
Teen Suicide
UFOs
The United Nations
U.S. Policy Toward China
Violent Children
Voting Behavior
Welfare Reform
What Is a Hate Crime?

IS MEDIA VIOLENCE A PROBLEM?

James D. Torr, *Book Editor*

Daniel Leone, *Publisher*
Bonnie Szumski, *Editorial Director*
Scott Barbour, *Managing Editor*

An Opposing Viewpoints® Series

Greenhaven Press, Inc.
San Diego, California

Library of Congress Cataloging-in-Publication Data

Is media violence a problem? / James D. Torr, book editor.
        p. cm. — (At issue)
    Includes bibliographical references and index.
    ISBN 0-7377-0802-6 (pbk. : alk. paper) —
ISBN 0-7377-0803-4 (lib. : alk. paper)
    1. Mass media and children. 2. Mass media and teenagers.
3. Violence in mass media. 4. Children and violence. I. Torr,
James D., 1974– II. At issue (San Diego, Calif.)

HQ784.M3 I8   2002
302.23'083—dc21   2001040407
                                                                    CIP

© 2002 by Greenhaven Press, Inc., PO Box 289009,
San Diego, CA 92198-9009

Printed in the U.S.A.

Table of Contents

Page

Introduction   6

1. Media Violence Harms Children   10
   American Academy of Child and Adolescent Psychiatry

2. Research on the Effects of Media Violence on Children   13
   Is Inconclusive
   Maggie Cutler

3. Violence on Television Is a Serious Problem   18
   James T. Hamilton

4. Violence on Television News Programs Is a Serious Problem   24
   Rita Colorito

5. The Problem of Television Violence Is Exaggerated   30
   Jib Fowles

6. Violence in the Movies Is a Serious Problem   40
   Robert W. Butler

7. Violence in Video Games Is a Serious Problem   44
   Eugene F. Provenzo Jr.

8. The Problem of Video Game Violence Is Exaggerated   49
   Greg Costikyan

9. The Glamorization of Guns in Rap Music Is a   58
   Serious Problem
   Jay Nordlinger

10. The Problem of Violent Themes in Popular Music   63
    Is Exaggerated
    Hillary B. Rosen

11. Media Violence Makes People More Violent   69
    Gregg Easterbrook

12. The Entertainment Industry Markets Violent Media   77
    to Children
    Charlie Condon

13. The Problem of Media Violence Is Not Serious Enough to   82
    Justify Censorship
    Wendy Kaminer

Organizations to Contact   86

Bibliography   89

Index   92

Introduction

On April 20, 1999, two teenagers armed with semiautomatic weapons and explosives killed thirteen people at Columbine High School in Littleton, Colorado. The teenagers, both students at Columbine, then took their own lives. The high school massacre in Littleton came in the wake of other school shootings. In 1997 in Pearl, Mississippi, a sixteen-year-old killed two students while in 1998 in Jonesboro, Arkansas, two middle school students killed four students and a teacher and wounded fifteen others. Sadly, the carnage did not end with the Littleton shooting. Just a month after Columbine, a fifteen-year-old wounded six students at a high school in Georgia; in May 2000, a seventh-grader shot a teacher at a Florida middle school; and in March 2001, a fifteen-year-old boy opened fire at a high school in Santee, California, killing two students and injuring thirteen others.

This seeming epidemic of school shootings has raised the level of public debate about a number of issues. Since all of the killers used firearms, many blamed the school shootings on the widespread availability of guns. Because most of the shooters were unpopular boys who had been rejected and in some cases tormented by their schoolmates, others have focused on the problem of bullying and peer-to-peer abuse in America's schools. However, since guns and bullying have always been problems with many of America's troubled youth, others looked beyond the obvious, pointing an accusing finger at the level of violence in the media. Could higher levels of violence in the media be what's pushing some troubled students to commit violence?

What the research shows

The idea that media violence may cause some people, particularly young people, to commit violence is not new. Parents have been concerned about violence on television almost since the medium's inception, and researchers have been studying television's effects on viewers for nearly as long. A 1993 report from the American Psychological Association (APA) summarized the research this way:

> There is absolutely no doubt that higher levels of viewing violence on television are correlated with increased acceptance of aggressive attitudes and increased aggressive behavior. Children's exposure to violence in the mass media, particularly at young ages, can have harmful lifelong consequences.

The APA stopped short of stating that media violence *causes* aggressive or violent behavior. Instead the consensus among the scientific community is that there is a *correlation* between the two. In his book *The Case for Tele-*

6

vision *Violence*, communication professor Jib Fowles points out that "correlational studies can never escape the fact that correlations are not causes." He cites researcher David Buckingham, who notes that "one may well discover that children who are violent watch a lot of television violence, but this does not prove that violent television causes real-life violence."

This problem has plagued research on media violence. In a 2001 report on youth violence, Surgeon General David Satcher did not include media violence as a major causal factor in youth violence. When asked why not, he explained that "it was extremely difficult to distinguish between the relatively small long-term effects of exposure to media violence and those of other influences." In other words, it is almost impossible for researchers to determine whether a given individual is violent because of media violence or because of other factors, such as substance abuse, childhood trauma, or having violent and/or antisocial parents.

Common sense

Therefore critics of media violence often emphasize the APA's second statement—that children's exposure to media violence "can have harmful lifelong consequences." In the debate over the Columbine school shootings, for example, the idea that a single violent film or video game made Eric Harris and Dylan Klebold into killers seems ludicrous. Yet the idea that a lifetime of violent films and video games may have contributed to their emotional instability seems like common sense. As *The Nation*'s Katherine Pollitt reasons, "whether or not you can connect this cultural effluvia [media violence] to specific acts of violence in a one-on-one causal way, thousands of hours of it can't be good for the soul."

This is the approach that the 1994–1997 National Television Violence Study took: Instead of trying to prove that television violence causes real-life violence, the study focused on other harmful effects associated with viewing television violence. Among these effects, according to the study are:

1) *"Learning of aggressive behaviors and attitudes."* Media violence may not make children violent, but it may teach them that violence is a normal way of solving problems.

2) *"Desensitization to violence."* This is the classic problem that horror movies face: Violence and gore may shock viewers initially, but they eventually become used to it. And heavy viewers of media violence may be less shocked by real-life violence.

3) *"Fear of being victimized by violence."* Constant exposure to violence in the media may lead people to believe that violence is everywhere and that they should be afraid. Researcher George Gerbner has described this as "Mean World Syndrome."

The pervasiveness of television

Researchers have long focused on television violence because television is the most pervasive format for media violence. Television has provided American children access to endless hours of increasingly violent programming that simply did not exist before the 1950s. Many schoolchildren spend more time watching television than they do doing homework or playing with friends. Because of this, it has been estimated that the average American will witness approximately 20,000 simulated television deaths in his or her lifetime. The sheer pervasiveness of television leads Mary Ann Watson, the author of *Defining Visions: Television and the American Experience Since 1945*, to conclude that saying "if you don't like what's on TV, just turn it off" is like saying "if you're troubled by air pollution, just stop breathing."

In 1996, the argument that television violence is too pervasive led Congress to pass the Telecommunications Act, which required television broadcasters to develop a voluntary ratings system for TV programs. The act also required television manufacturers to include the V-chip, an electronic device that allows parents to block out any program with a particular rating, in all new television sets made after 2000.

Other media

After the Columbine school shootings, attention shifted from television to other media, including movies, music, and video games. Movies have always been more violent than television, in part because movies are seen as a medium to which children have less access. In the 1990s, however, several movies were singled out in the media violence debate. Many critics felt that Quentin Tarantino's 1994 movie *Pulp Fiction* glorified the hitman lifestyle of its main characters. After Columbine, many pundits argued that 1995's *The Basketball Diaries*, which featured a daydream sequence in which the main character imagines gunning down students and teachers in his high school, may have influenced Eric Harris and Dylan Klebold. In his book *Screening Violence*, Stephen Prince argues that irresponsible portrayals of violence in the movies are on the rise. "Many filmmakers who portray ultraviolence are emotionally disengaged from it and show it in a dispassionate manner," he writes, "for them, it is a special effect and a box-office asset."

The charge that entertainers use violence as a gimmick to attract and captivate audiences has been leveled at the music industry as well as television and movies. In the early 1990s "gangsta" rap came under attack for its glorification of guns and gang life, and many rap and hip hop artists are still criticized for using violent and misogynistic themes in their lyrics. After Columbine, critics also accused "shock rocker" Marilyn Manson, as well as "goth" music in general, of promoting nihilism and despair. Thomas L. Jipping, director of a conservative think tank in Washington, D.C., writes that "negative or destructive themes [in popular music] are now the rule rather than the exception. . . . Popular music remains part of the cultural virus that can lead some young people to violence."

A final form of entertainment that has often been singled out as a "cultural virus" is the video game. As with other media, not all video games are violent, but some video games do center around violence. The most violent genre is that of the first-person shooter, which essentially simulates the shootouts that are so prominent in violent films and television. First-person shooters such as Doom and Quake were drawn into the media violence debate after it was reported that the shooters at Columbine High School had played them. Conservative columnist John Leo writes, "If we want to avoid more Littleton-style massacres, we will begin taking the social effects of [these] killing games more seriously."

Does violent entertainment have benefits?

Are these attacks on violent television, movies, music, and video games warranted? Many observers of the media violence debate feel that the hysteria over school shootings has gone too far. As horrific as they are, school shootings remain an extremely rare crime. Moreover, Mike Males, the author of *The Scapegoat Generation: America's War on Adolescents*, notes that "the best evidence shows that rates of murder, school violence, drug abuse, criminal arrest, violent death and gun fatality among middle- and upper-class teenagers have declined over the last 15 to 30 years. . . . If pop culture, music, video games, and Internet images affect teenagers, we should credit them for the fact that young people are behaving better," he concludes.

According to one theory, viewing media violence is a catharsis which may actually help reduce aggression. Violent entertainment may offer viewers—especially young males—a way to explore their violent tendencies without hurting anyone. In the case of violent video games, for example, New Jersey teenager Joe Stavitsky wrote in *Harper's* magazine that "as a 'geek,' I can tell you that . . . video games do not cause violence; they prevent it. We see games as a perfectly safe release from a physically violent reaction to the daily abuse leveled at us." Richard Rhodes, the author of *Why They Kill*, writes that "entertainment media are therapeutic, not toxic. That's what the evidence shows."

Although themes of violence have always played a part in storytelling, never before have young people been exposed to so many television shows, movies, songs, and video games that feature violence. For obvious reasons, the wave of school shootings has served to bring this issue to the fore. The authors featured in *At Issue: Is Media Violence a Problem?* present all sides of this important debate.

1

Media Violence Harms Children

American Academy of Child and Adolescent Psychiatry

The American Academy of Child and Adolescent Psychiatry is a national professional medical association representing over 6,500 child and adolescent psychiatrists. The AACAP issued the following joint statement in conjunction with the American Academy of Pediatrics, the American Psychological Association, and the American Medical Association.

Media violence is certainly not the sole or the most important factor contributing to youth violence, nor is censorship of violent media an effective solution to the problem. Nevertheless, numerous studies point to a causal connection between violent entertainment and aggressive behavior in children. Media violence can harm children in several ways: 1) by conditioning them to accept violence as a way of settling conflicts, 2) by desensitizing them toward real-life violence, 3) by making them more afraid that they will become victims of violence, and 4) by causing them to commit real-life violence.

We, the undersigned, represent the public health community. As with any community, there exists a diversity of viewpoints—but with many matters, there is also consensus. Although a wide variety of viewpoints on the import and impact of entertainment violence on children may exist outside the public health community, within it, there is a strong consensus on many of the effects on children's health, well-being and development.

Television, movies, music, and interactive games are powerful learning tools, and highly influential media. The average American child spends as much as 28 hours a week watching television, and typically at least an hour a day playing video games or surfing the Internet. Several more hours each week are spent watching movies and videos, and listening to music. These media can, and often are, used to instruct, encourage, and even inspire. But when these entertainment media showcase violence—and particularly in a context which glamorizes or trivializes it—the lessons learned can be destructive.

From The American Academy of Child and Adolescent Psychiatry's "Joint Statement on the Impact of Entertainment Violence on Children—Congressional Public Health Summit," July 26, 2000. Used with permission of Lippincott, Williams & Wilkins.

There are some in the entertainment industry who maintain that 1) violent programming is harmless because no studies exist that prove a connection between violent entertainment and aggressive behavior in children, and 2) young people know that television, movies, and video games are simply fantasy. Unfortunately, they are wrong on both counts.

Viewing entertainment violence can lead to increases in aggressive attitudes, values and behavior, particularly in children.

At this time, well over 1000 studies—including reports from the Surgeon General's office, the National Institute of Mental Health, and numerous studies conducted by leading figures within our medical and public health organizations—our own members—point overwhelmingly to a causal connection between media violence and aggressive behavior in some children. The conclusion of the public health community, based on over 30 years of research, is that viewing entertainment violence can lead to increases in aggressive attitudes, values and behavior, particularly in children.

Its effects are measurable and long-lasting. Moreover, prolonged viewing of media violence can lead to emotional desensitization toward violence in real life.

The effect of entertainment violence on children is complex and variable. Some children will be affected more than others. But while duration, intensity, and extent of the impact may vary, there are several measurable negative effects of children's exposure to violent entertainment. These effects take several forms.

- Children who see a lot of violence are more likely to view violence as an effective way of settling conflicts. Children exposed to violence are more likely to assume that acts of violence are acceptable behavior.
- Viewing violence can lead to emotional desensitization towards violence in real life. It can decrease the likelihood that one will take action on behalf of a victim when violence occurs.
- Entertainment violence feeds a perception that the world is a violent and mean place. Viewing violence increases fear of becoming a victim of violence, with a resultant increase in self-protective behaviors and a mistrust of others.
- Viewing violence may lead to real life violence. Children exposed to violent programming at a young age have a higher tendency for violent and aggressive behavior later in life than children who are not so exposed.

Although less research has been done on the impact of violent interactive entertainment (video games and other interactive media) on young people, preliminary studies indicate that the negative impact may be significantly more severe than that wrought by television, movies, or music. More study is needed in this area, and we urge that resources and attention be directed to this field.

We in no way mean to imply that entertainment violence is the sole, or even necessarily the most important factor contributing to youth aggression, anti-social attitudes, and violence. Family breakdown, peer influences, the availability of weapons, and numerous other factors may all contribute to these problems. Nor are we advocating restrictions on creative activity. The purpose of this document is descriptive, not prescriptive: we seek to lay out a clear picture of the pathological effects of entertainment violence. But we do hope that by articulating and releasing the consensus of the public health community, we may encourage greater public and parental awareness of the harms of violent entertainment, and encourage a more honest dialogue about what can be done to enhance the health and well-being of America's children.

Clarice Kestenbaum, MD
President
American Academy of Child and Adolescent Psychiatry

Donald E. Cook, MD
President
American Academy of Pediatrics

L. Michael Honaker, Ph.D.
Deputy Chief Executive Officer
American Psychological Association

Dr. E. Ratcliffe Anderson, Jr., MD
Executive Vice President
American Medical Association

Research on the Effects of Media Violence on Children Is Inconclusive

Maggie Cutler

Maggie Cutler is the author, at Nerve.com, of a biweekly column enti-
tled "The Secret Life of Maggie Cutler," which satirizes the confusion
between politics, media, and sex in American culture.

Thousands of studies have tried to determine how media violence affects children. However, all this research has produced no clear answers, and statements about "what the research shows" often exaggerate the actual evidence. It's almost impossible to separate media violence from all the other factors that can influence violent behavior. One thing that most researchers agree on is that real-life experiences are far more important than media violence in determining whether children commit violence.

Will girls imitate the new, kickass heroines in the Japanese anime *Cardcaptors?* Will the impressionable 12-year-olds exposed to trailers for MGM's *Disturbing Behavior* forever after associate good teen behavior with lobotomies? Did Nine Inch Nails and the video game *Doom* inspire the Trenchcoat Mafia's bloodbath at Columbine? Thousands of studies have been done to try to answer variants of the question: Does media violence lead to real-life violence, making children more antisocial and aggressive?

Too complex to study conclusively

Like most complex issues, discussions about the impact of media violence on children suffer from that commonest of media problems: fudge. Almost any simple statement on the subject obscures the complexity of the facts, half-facts and "results suggest" findings of the past forty years. The right-wing Parents Television Council, for example, announces that the per-hour rate in the United States of sexual and violent material and coarse language combined almost tripled from 1989 to 1999. But while PTC president Brent Bozell castigates the media for lowering standards of acceptable speech and behavior, he doesn't mention that in the final years of this avalanche of dreck the juvenile crime rate dropped more than 30 percent. Or, again, in August 1999 the Senate Judiciary Committee, headed by Orrin Hatch, reported confidently that "Television alone is responsible for 10 percent of youth violence." Given the overall juvenile crime count in 1997, the report implied, some 250 murders and 12,100 other violent crimes would not have been committed if it weren't for the likes of *Batman Beyond*.

But this, of course, is deeply misleading. One of the reasons so many media violence studies have been done is that the phenomenon may be too complex to study conclusively. There's no way, after all, to lock two clones in a black box, feed them different TV, movie and video-game diets and open the box years later to determine that, yes, it was definitely those Bruce Lee epics that turned clone A into Jesse Ventura, while clone B's exposure to the movie *Babe* produced a Pee Wee Herman.

Almost any simple statement on [the effects of media violence] obscures the complexity of the facts, half-facts and "results suggest" findings of the past forty years.

It has been hard, in other words, for media violence studies to shake the ambiguity of correlations. Several studies have shown that violent boys tend to watch more TV, choose more violent content and get more enjoyment out of it. But the studies admittedly can't show exactly how or why that happens. Do temperamentally violent kids seek out shows that express feelings they already have, or are they in it for the adrenaline boost? Do the sort of parents who let kids pig out on gore tend to do more than their share of other hurtful things that encourage violent behavior? To what extent is violent media producing little Johnny's aggression—or inspiring it, making it appear glamorous, righteous, acceptably gratuitous, fun or "normal"—and to what extent is it merely satisfying little Johnny's greater-than-average longings for the mayhem, vengeance, superhuman power and sweet revenge that most people, at times, secretly crave?

One of many risk factors

According to James Garbarino, author of *Lost Boys: Why Our Sons Turn Violent and How We Can Save Them*, it makes no sense to talk about violent media as a direct cause of youth violence. Rather, he says, "it depends": Media violence is a risk factor that, working in concert with others, can exacerbate bad behavior.

Like Orrin Hatch's committee, Garbarino estimates the effect of violent media on juvenile violence at about 10 percent, but his ecology-of-violence formulation is far less tidy than the Hatch committee's pop-psych model. Garbarino himself reports in an e-mail that he would like to see media violence treated as a public health problem—dammed at its

Hollywood source the way sewage treatment plants "reduce the problem of cholera." Nevertheless, his ecology model of how juvenile violence emerges from complex, interacting factors means that hyperaggressive, "asset poor" kids are likely to be harmed by graphic depictions of violence, while balanced, "asset rich" kids are likely to remain unscathed. A few studies have even found that a "cathartic effect" of media violence makes some kids less aggressive. This wide range of individual variance makes policy prescriptions a tricky matter.

Violent media [is] only one among many factors in juvenile violence.

The American Psychological Association's Commission on Violence and Youth (1994) mentions violent media as only one among many factors in juvenile violence. It stresses that inborn temperament, early parental abuse or neglect, poverty, cognitive impairment, plus a deficiency of corrective influences or role models in various combinations will put a child at greater risk for violence, both as perpetrator and as victim. The APA found that many damaged kids' lives can be salvaged with early intervention. By the age of 8, these at-risk kids can be identified. Once identified they can be taught skills that enable them to resolve conflicts peacefully. The APA adds that parental guidance along with reducing kids' exposure to graphic violence can help keep them out of the correctional system. But for the kids most at risk, reducing representational violence is obviously no cure. So this past fall [2000], when Senators John McCain and Joseph Lieberman ordered the entertainment industry to stop advertising its nastier products to young children or else face (shudder) regulation, it was fair of media critics to castigate them for exploiting the media violence problem for its bipartisan glow rather than attempting to find the least coercive, most effective ways of keeping children safe and sane.

Defining "violent"

Perhaps the biggest problem in mitigating the effect of media violence on children is that it's hard to nail down just what "violent media" means to actual kids. As with adult pornography, we all think we know what it is until we have to define it. That's because kids not only process content differently depending on their temperament, background and circumstances, they seem to process it differently at different ages, too.

A series of often-cited studies known as Winick and Winick (1979) charted distinct stages in media processing abilities. Fairly early, from about 6 until about 10, most—but not all—kids are learning to deal with media much as adults do: interactively rather than passively. In her 1985 book, *Watching Dallas: Soap Opera and the Melodramatic Imagination,* Ien Ang of the University of Western Sydney in Australia showed that different adult viewers rewrote the "messages" of shows to suit their own views. So a wise little girl whose parents discuss media with her might enjoy Wrestlemania as an amusing guide to crazy-guys-to-avoid, while an angry, abandoned, slow-witted child is more likely to enter its world of insult and injury with uncritical awe.

At first blush, measures like content labeling would seem to make more sense for the 2-to-6 set because young kids do get confused about reality, fantasy, information and advertising. But again, what constitutes "violent" content isn't always obvious. The Winicks found that young children whose parents fought a lot responded with more distress to representations of people yelling and screaming—because it seemed real—than to blatant violence for which they had no frame of reference. Should there be a label for "loud and emotional"? And if so, should we slap it on *La Boheme?*

Because representational violence is so hard to define, the recently reported Stanford media effects studies, which focused on third and fourth graders, ducked the problem. The study team, headed by Thomas Robinson, simply worked with teachers, parents and kids to help children lower their overall media use voluntarily. As a result of the six-month program, which involved classroom instruction, parental support and peer pressure, kids used media about 30 percent less than usual. And, they found, verbal and physical aggression levels subsequently dropped 25 percent on average. These numbers are being taken especially seriously because they were established "in the field" rather than in the lab, so that the verbal and physical aggression measured was actual, not simulated by, say, asking a child to kick or insult a doll. As media violence studies predicted, the more aggressive kids were to begin with, the more their behavior improved when they consumed less of whatever it was they normally consumed.

---

*It's hard to nail down just what "violent media"
means to actual kids.*

Although the Stanford study—perhaps to stay popular with granters—is being promoted as a study on media violence, it is really a study of media overuse, self-awareness and the rewards of self-discipline. Its clearest finding wasn't that media violence is always harmful but that too much mediated experience seems to impair children's ability to interact well with other people. Follow-up studies at Stanford will show whether the remarkable benefits of its media reduction program last over a longer period. If they do, such classes may be a helpful addition to school curriculums in conjunction, perhaps, with courses in conflict resolution. But in any case, its results demonstrate less the effects of specific content than what could be called "the rule of the real."

Real life has more impact than fantasy violence

The rule of the real says that however strong media influences may be, real life is stronger. Real love, real money, real political events and real-life, unmediated interpersonal experience all shape kids' lives, minds and behavior more powerfully than any entertainment products. Even media seen or understood as real—news, documentaries, interviews—will have more impact than that which a kid knows is make-believe. As the Winicks found, kids understand early that cartoon violence is a joke, not a model. Even wrestling, once kids figure out that it's staged, gets processed differently from, say, a schoolyard beating.

Without belittling the importance of media research, it's time that the rule of the real governed policy as well. After all, boys whose dads do hard time tend to end up in jail, while boys who see *Fight Club* tend to end up in film clubs; it's more likely that the Santana High killer decided to shoot up his school after seeing the anniversary coverage of Columbine than because he watched *The Mummy*. Abused young women don't kill their battering husbands because they grew up watching *Charlie's Angels*, and teens who hear no criticism of the Gulf War tend to want another. Given limited energies and resources, if our politicians really wanted to reduce youth violence, they would push to reform prison policies, provide supervised after-school activities for teens and get early, comprehensive help to high-risk children. As a community, we would do better to challenge the corporate conglomeration of news outlets than to legislate the jugs 'n' jugular quotient in *Tomb Raider*, its labeling or ad placements—and this is true even though the stuff kids like is often quite nasty, and even though the better part of the scientific establishment now agrees that such excitements are less than benign. But setting priorities like these is hard because, while the real may rule children's lives as it rules our own, it's much more fun to imagine controlling their dreams.

3

Violence on Television Is a Serious Problem

James T. Hamilton

James T. Hamilton is a professor of public policy, economics, and polit-
ical science at Duke University and the author of Channeling Violence: The Economic Market for Violent Television Programming.

Television programmers and advertisers purposely feature violence in their programming to attract viewers—mostly males ages
eighteen to thirty-four. In doing so they unintentionally expose
children to adult-themed violence. In this respect, TV violence is
similar to the problem of pollution: The manufacturers of this
toxic violence do not intend to harm society with it, but neither
do they take responsibility for its effects. Communities and the
government must take action to limit the harmful effects that this
industrial pollution has on children's cultural environment.

Editor's note: The following remarks were presented to the Senate Committee on
Commerce, Science, and Transportation at a May 18, 1999, hearing on televi-
sion violence.

I am James T. Hamilton, an associate professor of public policy, economics, and political science at Duke University. I appreciate the opportunity to testify before your committee, since my work on television
violence was initially inspired by a congressional debate. During the mid-
1990s, Congress considered "report card" legislation that would have developed information on program content and compiled a list of advertisers that supported violent programming. At the time I was studying how
companies react to information provision about their pollution records
under the Environmental Protection Agency's Toxics Release Inventory
program. Thinking about toxics and television violence, I came to view
both as situations where the choices of producers do not reflect the full
costs to society of their actions. Both situations involve market failures
that economists call negative externalities, since the negative impacts on
society arising from production are external to the decision making of

From James T. Hamilton's statement before the Senate Committee on Commerce, Science, and
Transportation, May 18, 1999.

manufacturers. That insight led me to write a recently published book entitled *Channeling Violence: The Economic Market for Violent Television Programming* (Princeton University Press, 1998). This morning I hope to describe the economics behind television violence and the implications of economic reasoning for policies to address it.

Violent images are more likely to be imitated if they go unpunished, show little pain or suffering, and involve attractive perpetrators.

Television violence is at its core a problem of pollution. Programmers and advertisers use violent content to target television's most valuable demographic, viewers age 18–34. The executives who schedule violence to garner ratings and profits do not take into account the full impact on society of their actions. Research shows that television violence does increase levels of aggression, fear, and desensitization among some who consume it. The strongest impacts are on the youngest viewers. Children are not the target of advertisers on most violent programs. But their exposure to violent images can lead to social damages not factored into decisions about when to air programs and where to draw the line on content.

Common defenses of television violence

In writing a book on the market for violent programming, I (understandably) found few people in the entertainment industry willing to agree their products generate cultural pollution. Media officials often deflect criticisms of their programs with a standard set of responses, which I came to view as the "Top 5 Reasons Why TV Violence Is Not a Problem."

1. *We use violence on television to tell, not sell, stories.* Television executives link the use of violence to narrative needs. In hearings before Congress, network executives have denied that they use violence to earn ratings. Yet I found in my research on programming strategies that every channel type uses violence to gain viewers:

- During the sweeps periods, the four major broadcast networks were much more likely to air movies that deal with murder, focus on tales of family crime, and feature family crime or murder stories based on real-life incidents. Nearly a third of network movies during sweeps periods dealt with murder. The Fox network, which often aired movies starting at 8 PM, increased its use of violent movies from 42% to 84% during sweeps.
- When ABC aired *Monday Night Football,* the basic cable channel TBS dropped its use of violent movies on Monday nights. The percentage of violent movies declined on this channel from 92% to 65% of the films shown. When football season ended and male viewers were up for grabs, the violent movies returned.
- When *Seinfeld* dominated ratings on Thursday evenings, HBO had a strategy known internally as 'Testosterone Thursday,' in which it programmed low-quality violent films at 9 PM to attract male viewers uninterested in *Seinfeld.*

These strategic uses of violent programs all contradict the frequent claims that violence is not used to attract viewers.

2. *Violence on television is a reflection of violence in society.* Analyzing data across the country on local news content, I found that the percentage of stories devoted to crime and the percentage of lead stories dealing with crime were not related to the crime rate in a city. Rather it was audience interest in crime, reflected by ratings for *Cops* in the market, that predicted the degree local news directors focused on crime in their newscasts. The stronger the audience interest in reality police show programming, the more likely newscasts in an area were to focus on crime.

3. *Images on television do not influence behavior.* Social science research indicates that violent images are more likely to be imitated if they go unpunished, show little pain or suffering, and involve attractive perpetrators. This describes the types of violence often used on television. (For statistical evidence on the context of violence in television, see the work by the National Television Violence Study researchers in *Television Violence and Public Policy*, James T. Hamilton, editor).

4. *Television is less violent today.* It is true that on primetime network broadcast television, the percentage of programs in violent genres has dropped in the 1990s. In 1984 51% of primetime network series were in violent genres, a figure that declined to 23% in 1993. But violence has simply migrated to basic and premium cable channels. Nearly two thirds of all basic cable movies on at 8 PM on weekdays are violent. Of the top 5 programs viewed each week on premium channels, over half are violent movies.

Violence is used in high-quality films. Yet these types of movies are only a small percentage of those shown on television.

---

5. *What about* Schindler's List? Violence is used in high-quality films. Yet these types of movies are only a small percentage of those shown on television. In a sample of 5,000 violent movies on broadcast, basic cable, and premium channels, I found that only 3% were given four stars (the highest rating) by critics.

A pollution problem

In opinion surveys about television, the majority of adult respondents indicates that there is too much violence in entertainment programming. Yet there are segments of viewers who enjoy and consume violent shows. Males age 18–34 are the top consumers of violent entertainment fare, followed by females 18–34. These viewers are particularly prized by advertisers, in part because their purchase decisions can be more easily influenced than those of older consumers. As a result, programmers often target these young adults and use violent shows to attract them. These same violent programs may also attract an unintended audience, children 2–11 and teens 12–17. Primetime shows do not get higher ad rates for attracting child viewers, since the products on these programs are aimed at adults. Yet because the programs are on when children are in the viewing audience (nearly 1 out of 3 children and teens are watching television at 8 PM on weekdays), children see violent shows aimed at adults.

This exposure of children to violent programs generates a pollution problem. Research indicates that some children who consume violent programming are more likely to become aggressive, to feel desensitized to violence, or experience fear upon viewing. While the market for violence works well in delivering a segment of adult viewers what they want, the market fails with respect to shielding children from harmful effects. Neither advertisers nor programmers are led to consider the full costs to society of using violence to attract viewers, since they are not led by the market to internalize in their decision making the negative impacts these programs have on children. The result—too much violence consumed by too many children.

Neither advertisers nor programmers are led to consider the full costs to society of using violence to attract viewers.

Broadcasters correctly stress that their business is selling audiences to advertisers, not raising or educating children. When they make programming choices, they focus on the number of viewers, the value of these viewers to advertisers, the cost of programs, and the number of competitors offering different types of fare. There are multiple incentives that favor the provision of violent programming by some channels. Violent shows are cheaper for networks to purchase. Violent programs are twice as likely to be exported, which increases the returns to producers. As the number of viewing options increases, channels serving particular niches continue to grow—including those that specialize in developing a brand name for violence. The proliferation of channels will involve an increase in the number of violent viewing options and the intensity of violence on some channels.

If violence on television is a pollution problem, what is to be done? In dealing with everyday pollutants such as toxic chemicals released into the air, the government has a wide array of policy tools to reduce the harms created: zoning of noxious facilities; the direct control of the release of chemicals; the use of liability laws to change behavior; and the taxing of polluting activities. In the media realm the First Amendment rightfully restricts the policy options available to deal with television violence. However, I do believe that there are at least three steps which industry, encouraged by government, can take to lower the exposure of children: provide accurate content information; consider the likely number of children in the audience when scheduling; and take responsibility for the potential harms that arise from some types of programs.

Parents need help

Information Provision. Parents make the ultimate decisions about whether their children will consume violent content. Yet even for the parents most concerned about shielding their children, the costs in terms of time of finding out what programs contain potentially objectionable content, ascertaining when particular programs are on, and monitoring the viewing of their children are extensive. The V-chip and program ratings provided by the television industry offer the potential to reduce the costs to parents of being responsible parents. The V-chip and ratings system will only work, however, if parents believe the system is credible, informative, and effective.

In my research I found that parents do act if provided with program content information. I found that on primetime broadcast network movies, the Nielsen rating for children 2–11 dropped by about 14% on movies that carried a viewer discretion warning. Since these movies were averaging 1.6 million children 2–11 in their audiences, the drop in viewing translated into approximately 220,000 fewer children in the audience for a movie carrying a warning. The warnings had no impact on ratings for teens or adults. But the warnings did change the willingness of some advertisers to sponsor a program. Once a warning was placed on a violent theatrical film shown on network movies, products likely to experience harm to their brand images by being associated with violence were less likely to advertise on the movie. In particular, products consumed by women, by older viewers, and by families with children were less likely to advertise on a movie once it carried a viewer discretion warning. The number of general product ads on a movie also dropped slightly when the warning was placed. Products aimed at men and younger adults were actually more willing to advertise on these movies with warnings, since their consumers report they are less likely to see television violence as a problem. The companies advertising on movies with warnings were those at less risk for brand name damage.

Violent shows are cheaper for networks to purchase.

Controversy about content can have a large impact on advertisers. I found that in its first season, ads on *NYPD Blue* sold at a 45% discount because of the initial unwillingness of advertisers to be associated with the program. Broadcasters are reluctant to provide viewers with content information in part because of the fear that this will generate controversy and change the willingness of advertisers to support a particular program. Cable channels have historically provided much more detailed content descriptors for their programs, in part because they are less dependent on advertiser reactions. During the early implementation of the television rating system, I found evidence that continued concern for advertiser reactions kept the broadcast networks from providing accurate program indicators on more controversial programs. Comparing the ratings provided by the networks with program evaluations from the Parents' Television Council, I found that the networks frequently "underlabeled" programs, such as giving a program found by the parents' viewing group to contain "gratuitous sex, explicit dialogue, violent content, or obscene language" a TV-PG rating rather than a TV-14 rating. The networks were more likely to underlabel the programs with higher ad rates. Among the networks, NBC had the highest ad rates on underlabeled programs.

More recent research by Dale Kunkel and colleagues (*An Assessment of the Television Industry's Use of V-chip Ratings*) indicates that over three fourths of programs with violence did not carry a violence indicator. An obvious first step that industry officials can take to reduce the exposure of children to violent content is to label such content more frequently, though they may be reluctant to do this because of fears of advertiser backlash. The impact of improved labeling will take time to develop, since the current rating system is akin to the provision of software without hardware. As sets with V-chips arrive in the market, parents will be able to use the content rating systems more easily.

The industry must be more responsible

Scheduling. A second measure that industry officials could take would be to shift violent programming to times when children are less likely to be in the audience. This would require a substantial change in behavior by some programmers, since the times when children and teens are in the audience are often the same times when viewers 18–34 are in the audience. At 8 PM on weekdays, for example, nearly one out of three children and teens is watching television. At this time, nearly two thirds of all movies on basic cable are violent. Fox, which broadcast the highest percentage of violent films among the major networks, often began its movies at 8 PM. Early evening and daytime hours on weekends are also a frequent time period for the programming of syndicated violent shows. Half of the weekly exposures of children 2–11 to syndicated action adventure/crime series occurs on weekends during the day or early evening before 8 PM. If programmers were to shift violent content to hours where viewing by children was less likely to arise, this would reduce the probability that those most susceptible to harm were exposed to violent content.

Responsibility. A final measure that industry officials could adopt is to admit that some programs may be damaging for some children to watch. In debates about television violence, executives often deny the potential for harm to arise from programming. Parents will be more likely to act to shield their children from violent programming if there is a more consistent message about likely dangers. I found that parents who were personally bothered by television violence were much more likely to intervene and switch channels when objectionable content came on while children were viewing. Parent groups, educators, pediatricians, and foundations all have a role in alerting parents to the need to shield children from violent content and providing information on how to use options such as the ratings system and V-chip. Entertainment officials also have a role to play in this education process. The targeting and repetition of messages to change consumer decisions is the economic foundation of television programming. If the industry could add an additional message to the information it conveys, that violent content may be harmful and parents should shield their children from it, there may be a high pay off to society from this type of advertising.

4

Violence on Television News Programs Is a Serious Problem

Rita Colorito

Rita Colorito is a freelance writer who lives and works in Bloomington, Indiana.

Although rates of violent crime fell throughout most of the 1990s, television news coverage of violent crime rose. Television newsmagazines such as *20/20* and *Dateline* often feature stories on horrific crimes, sometimes showing grisly crime scene photos or frightening re-enactments of stalkings, rapes, and murders. By devoting so much coverage to murder, television newsmagazines give the false impression that violent crime is rampant. As a result, heavy viewers of TV news are more likely to be worried about becoming victims of crime themselves.

During the 1980s, sex sold everything from bar soap to underwear and even saturated the news. The American public heard ad nauseam of the sexual exploits of politicians, ministers, and movie stars. In addition, the sex lives of Joe and Jane Doe filtered into our homes courtesy not only of sensational TV talk shows but also the supposedly higher-brow television news shows and magazines.

Since the early 1990s, though, television news has expanded its fascination with the lurid and the lascivious to include the morbid and mutilated.

Although the evening news has always reported on stories of death by crime, war, and natural disaster, television newsmagazines have taken reporting on murder to a new level. Some nights you can't turn on one of these programs without hearing and watching a blow-by-blow description, literally, of how someone was murdered by a serial killer, an abusive husband, or armed high school students.

Scenes of the crime

"Justice for Sheila," on CBS's *48 Hours,* walked viewers through the murder scene through the words of Sheila's daughter, Stevie, who found her dead mother. As Stevie recalled rushing home to tell her mom good news, we see happy images of Sheila, her quadruple two-year-old boys, and their home.

When Stevie can't find Sheila, *48 Hours* follows her path through each room, and finally shows actual crime scene photos of the laundry room where her mother lay dead. Although the photos never show Sheila's entire body or mutilated head—we learn her throat had been slashed and her face shot—they do show the walls and floor covered with blood, and quick shots of Sheila's hands and bloody jeaned legs. That part of the segment ends with Stevie's hysterical 911 call.

Susan Zirinsky, *48 Hours'* executive producer, says she is sensitive to what material is shown. "We are conscious of the families that are watching," she states. "In the [Sheila] Belesh story, you never saw the entire body. You saw a hand or a knife. Almost like a fast image. We tend not to linger."

Television newsmagazines have taken reporting on murder to a new level.

ABC's *20/20 Downtown* didn't show the same reserve in its story on Teena Brandon, the girl who lived life as a boy and was murdered by former male friends when her secret was revealed. It showed actual photos of Brandon sprawled on the bed after being shot—first a closeup of her face with blood on it, then a wide shot of her body, blood spread across her chest. There were also photos of two other victims shot dead.

"We try to exercise taste and good judgment, whatever is appropriate," says Victor Neufeld, *20/20*'s executive producer. For TV newsmagazines, crime scene photos are merely part of the voyeuristic package.

When crime scene photos are lacking, the script supplies the grisly details. In "Burden of Proof," *NBC Dateline*'s story on Michael Skekel, the nephew of Ethel Kennedy accused of killing Martha Moxley in 1975, the murder is described graphically: "What did happen was savage. . . . The 15-year-old was bludgeoned to death by a golf club—a six-iron—the broken shaft of it jabbed through her neck."

In "Justice for Sheila," after Stevie recalls that "there was blood everywhere, even on the babies," the correspondent dramatically adds, "It was their mother's blood."

In September 1999, ABC's *20/20* devoted a full hour to recounting the killings of four women in Yosemite National Park by motel handyman and serial killer Cary Stayner. Elizabeth Vargas, *20/20*'s correspondent, didn't shed any new light as to why Stayner committed the murders. Except for a brief taped phone conversation, Vargas barely interviewed Stayner.

Instead, *20/20* took viewers through the last hours of each woman's life, in all their horrific, gory details, from how Stayner talked his way that night into the motel room of a woman, her daughter, and her friend, how he bound and gagged them, how he raped one and killed her, then another, then drove the daughter down a deserted road and stabbed her, to how he murdered another young woman, after she struggled bravely and almost escaped, to finally how Stayner slashed her throat so savagely he decapitated her.

"That's a detective story, what happened to these women," says Neufeld, *20/20's* executive producer. "Every media outlet did that story. That show was highly viewed."

Journalism versus entertainment

With the proliferation of cable channels, the Internet, and TV news-magazines—there's at least one on every night of the week—the need to compete for a shrinking viewership drives newsmagazines to produce true crime stories. To attract viewers, these stories often resemble violent feature films.

"News programs are shaped like a commercial product, and they use the same types of strategies that dominate programming later in the evening," says James Hamilton, author of *Channeling Violence: The Economic Market for Violent Television Programming.*

"Unfortunately, a lot of times this programming is portrayed in an exciting manner, a titillating manner. The reality is, what is so exciting and titillating about someone being murdered?" asks Sheryl Grana, associate professor of sociology at the University of Minnesota in Duluth.

Grana, who analyzes the graphicness of violent movies in her courses, agrees that newsmagazines emulate their entertainment counterparts. "People spend money at the movies, and newsmagazines notice that," says Grana. "Death and murder sell, and that's what they want to produce to make money."

Males aged 18 to 34 are the top viewers of violent television programming in general, says Hamilton. They are a valuable demographic because of the advertisers they attract. Higher ratings mean higher ad revenue.

To attract viewers, [television newsmagazine] stories often resemble violent feature films.

Neufeld argues that *20/20* airs only well-told journalistic endeavors. "We don't do entertainment—none of this is entertainment," he remarks. "This is reporting. In general, they are very compelling and very dramatic. They say a lot about human nature and shared experiences. They are emotional stories that reflect the strongest, most intimate parts of human nature."

Zirinsky says *48 Hours'* viewership is dramatically high for these segments. When deciding which true crime stories to air, she looks for a larger context or interesting elements, such as clever detective work. She recalls one story of a police officer who helped convict a young man of murder based on a single clothing thread.

"The crime was horrific, but solving the crime was terrific," she says.

She admits that not all stories are newsworthy. "I won't be dishonest," says Zirinsky. "Some stories have an appeal because of the bizarre nature of the crimes and the characters involved," citing "Murder in L.A.," a story of a socialite who murders her husband. But she says she rejects some crime stories because of their tawdry nature, because of police bumbling, or because the legal case wasn't particularly interesting.

"Because the national programmers have minute-by-minute Nielsen [ratings], they really know what sells and what doesn't," says Hamilton. Entertainment programmers have long known that law and order sells. Some of the networks' highest-rated dramas are set in court.

It took the O.J. Simpson murder trial for news programmers to realize the benefits. In June 1994, ABC, CBS, and NBC saw a 24 percent increase in their combined ratings during their coverage of the preliminary O.J. Simpson court hearing, and CNN's trial coverage added $25 million in revenue, according to *Advertising Age*.

Newsmagazines now capitalize on the public's interest in courtroom dramas. MSNBC thrives on the JonBenet Ramsey murder case. *Dateline* produces stories with Court TV, the 24-hour cable network it partially owns that airs taped and live trials in 41 states. *Dateline*/Court TV Interactive stories combine the crime and the trial with audience participation via E-mail, a sort of armchair jury.

In "Death in the Afternoon," which aired February 1, 2000, an ex-husband shot his wife 12 times at their daughter's graveside, blaming her for their daughter's suicide. The segment showed the actual shooting, captured by a local news crew, several times interspersed with video of the trial proceedings. More than 14,000 cyberjurists chose to convict him of murder. (*Dateline*'s executive producer declined to be interviewed.)

Except for *20/20*'s Stayner and Brandon stories, all the stories described revolved around a recent or upcoming trial. In January 2000, multimillionaire Alan Blackthorne, Sheila's ex-husband, was arrested for her murder: *48 Hours* had obtained the only television interview with him prior to his arrest. In *Dateline*'s "Death in the Afternoon," the trial began on January 19, 2000, and in its brief segment on Kennedy's nephew Skekel, the trial was set to begin the following day.

"People really find peeling the onion back on the judicial process fascinating," says Zirinsky. "That's what allows us to do this." She says she gets a lot of E-mail from people who are interested in the crimes and want to help solve them. The stories, she claims, help bring closure to the families involved and in several cases have led to cases being solved.

"It's an interesting compendium of science, legal work, and humanity," she says. "As a journalist, it's an amazing process to follow along. We want to take you along with us. These stories allow us to see the legal system work or not work."

Crime and consequences

Grana, who specializes in criminology, says newsmagazines often portray crime and its consequences inaccurately. "True crime stories are largely blown out of proportion and are misrepresentative of how murder is dealt with in the criminal justice system," she says. "Murder is the least common crime there is. Having your hubcaps ripped off is much more common, but we're not interested in that."

According to a 1998 U.S. Department of Justice report, the nation's murder rate had dropped to its lowest level in three decades, and violent crime had declined for the sixth year in a row and stood at its lowest level since 1987. Yet, from 1990 to 1995 network coverage of murder rose 336 percent—1,352 percent if you include the O.J. Simpson case, according to the Center for Media and Public Affairs (CMPA). And since 1992, crime has been one of the top three categories covered by the evening news shows of ABC, CBS, and NBC. During 1994 and 1995, the years of the O.J. case, crime was No. 1, says the CMPA.

While the number of violent entertainment programs on network television actually declined in the 1990s, crime stories rose in the news programs.

While the number of violent entertainment programs on network television actually declined in the 1990s, crime stories rose in the news programs. According to Chuck Whitney, professor of journalism at the University of Texas at Austin, who studied 526 reality-based programs over a three-year period for the National Television Violence Study, mass violence/warfare is the No. 1 category of violence in news and public affairs programming. A close second is murder.

"If you turn on local news, one out of three stories was going to be about crime," says Hamilton, who also serves as director of the Institute on Media Violence at Duke University. "And one out of three of those crime stories was about murder—averaging one murder story per every half-hour."

Showing the most extreme, yet rare violence in America leads to something researcher George Gerbner has called the "mean world syndrome."

"People who are heavier viewers [of violent news] tend to believe that the world is a more violent place," says Hamilton. "In surveys they are more likely to say they bought locks for their houses. And they are more likely to say that they are afraid of walking by themselves at night."

Whitney says the violence in TV newsmagazines, the most morbid of all reality-based programming, isn't of particular concern because it generally doesn't encourage aggression, instill fear, or cause desensitization. In fact, it's just the opposite.

"News and public affairs programming in particular tends to show violence in a not very glamorized, not very sanitized light," he says—perhaps the only good news about murder stories.

Same old, same old

Neufeld argues that coverage of true-crime stories is nothing new. "Police and crime stories are a long-standing tradition in journalism," he says. "There's always been big true crime and legal cases, from the Lindbergh trial, from the birth of civilization."

Carl Holmberg, a professor in the Department of Popular Culture at Bowling Green State University, agrees. "Since the Vietnam War, Americans have been acculturated to 'reality-based' programming called 'the news.' That Americans want more of such programming can be seen in the almost immediate popularity of CNN and CNN Headline News. There is only a small step to other, more tabloid sorts of journalism. In this sense, too, there has been a long history of sensational news in North America, originally via newspapers.

"Let's face it," he continues, "the truth is stranger than fiction. What could be more stunning and attention-getting than children killing people? We have boring leaders. Children, in extremity, are not boring. As long as television is for making money, we will be given this sort of failed vision of reality."

"It's a chicken-versus-egg phenomenon," argues Grana. "We are interested, but part of our interest comes from the media giving it to us."

So as long as death sells, we can expect to see more of the same.

The Problem of Television
Violence Is Exaggerated

Jib Fowles

Jib Fowles is a professor of communication at the University of Houston-Clear Lake and the author of The Case for Television Violence.

Because everyone has access to television, its use cannot be regulated—and therefore those who would like to control television see it as out of control and threatening. TV violence is an excuse for many groups to attack television. In the realm of culture, educated elites attack the violent programs that the masses enjoy. Whites worry that TV violence will increase crime rates among minorities. Older Americans feel that TV violence is common because it is popular among younger viewers, women blame its prevalence on men, and religious conservatives claim that the TV violence is foisted on them by liberals. TV violence is attacked because it is a forum for these larger social conflicts, not because it actually causes real-life violence.

Although television violence has never been shown to cause hostile behavior, its sinister reputation lives on. This is because the issue masks a variety of other struggles. Many of these conflicts are suppressed because they may pose a threat to social order or are considered unseemly topics for public discussion. Hence, we hear only the polite versions of the conflicts between races, genders, and generations, although these struggles roil national life. Because they are denied full expression, such conflicts are transferred into other debates, including and perhaps especially the issue of television violence.

Television violence is a whipping boy, a stand-in for other clashes, real or imagined. As one astute observer put it a few years back during a previous cycle of panic, "The debate about children and media violence is really a debate about other things, many of which have very little to do with the media."

There are several reasons why television violence has become such an exemplary whipping boy. First, it is a large target, present in one form or another in virtually every household in America. Second, if one puts on blinders, there might seem to be some correspondence between the mayhem on the television screen and real-life aggression; both televised entertainment and the real world deal in hostilities. Third and most important, television violence attracts no champions; the very idea of defending it seems silly to most people. Even industry representatives rarely get beyond conciliatory statements when they are compelled to address the matter. In one survey, 78 percent of entertainment industry executives expressed concern about the content of the action dramas they helped produce. In 1993 Ted Turner, perhaps the most conspicuous industry leader at the time, said in congressional testimony that television was "the single most important factor causing violence in America." The object of derision simply stands still and takes all the abuse that can be heaped on it.

What are the real conflicts that are being displaced? Most entail the stronger overwhelming the weaker, but in some conflicts the weaker retaliate through moral exertion. Here is a brief examination of the most important conflicts.

High vs. low

The attack on television violence is, at least in part, an attack by the upper classes and their partisans on popular culture. In this interpretation, which has been broached repeatedly for a quarter-century, the push to reform television is simply the latest manifestation of the struggle between the high and the low, the dominant and the dominated.

The United States is often regarded as a virtually classless society. Indeed, the overwhelming majority of Americans identify themselves as members of a "middle" class. Everyday experience, however, points in a different direction. Americans constantly make class judgments about one another. They quickly note outward appearances and speech patterns. When necessary, one person learns about the other's occupation and education, where he lives and what car he drives, and locates that person socially. Notions of class rank notoriously crop up in courtship and marriage. Characters in films and television programs radiate class information about themselves to audience members who know precisely how to read such clues.

The debate about children and media violence is really a debate about other things, many of which have very little to do with the media.

Perhaps the preeminent living theorist and researcher into matters of class and culture is Pierre Bourdieu. He is best known for his work on the segmentation of society according to preferences in aesthetic taste (for instance, going or not going to art museums). At the center of Bourdieu's work is the concept of habitus, an idea similar to that of the English word, habit. Habitus is the system of predispositions ingrained in a particular group or social class. It manifests itself in similar thoughts, behaviors, expressions, and leisure pursuits. The shared habitus unites and defines the social entity. Habitus, however, does not shackle individuals; in Bourdieu's scheme, there is ample room for idiosyncratic action.

The attack on television violence is, at least in part, an attack by the upper classes and their partisans on popular culture.

Another concept special to Bourdieu is capital, approximately equivalent to social power. In addition to conventional economic wealth, there are several other kinds of capital in Bourdieu's system. Cultural capital (preferences gained primarily through education), symbolic capital (prestige and honors), and social capital (whom one knows) work together with financial capital to define a person's location in the overall social structure. Social action then becomes a function of class habitus and personal capitals. A final term from Bourdieu's work is reproduction, which is the manner by which social classes reproduce themselves and, in doing so, preserve status differences. For Bourdieu, the reproduction of habitus is the key work of a social class.

Although Bourdieu does not discuss television in his magisterial work, *Distinctions* (1984), it does not take much imagination to extend his analysis. He writes in his opening pages that taste (cultural capital) functions as a marker of social class; therefore, different preferences (such as watching television violence or not) can be used to situate a person hierarchically. According to this system, an attack on the most popular medium, on television and especially its violent content, would also be an attack by the dominant class on the habitus of the dominated. To reconfirm social distinctions and maintain exclusivity, members of the dominant class need only profess an opposition to television violence. (Ironically, Bourdieu, mustering all the trappings of a French intellectual, himself attacked television in a series of lectures published in English in 1998, calling the medium "a threat to political life and to democracy itself.")

The "mass media"

In the derisive vocabulary of this dominant class, violent content is delivered via the "mass media." This term is used so much that it seems unremarkable, but repetition has concealed its derogatory nature. Programming is not received by an undifferentiated horde; it is received by individuals. In fact, there is no mass, there are no masses. As the cultural critic Raymond Williams wrote in 1958, "The masses are always the others, whom we don't know, and can't know. . . . Masses are other people. There are in fact no masses; there are only ways of seeing people as masses." When dominant Americans chastise the nonexistent phenomena of the "masses" and their "mass medium" of television, with its evil content, what they are really endeavoring is to disparage and suppress the culture of dominated Americans.

The class nature of this conflict is evident in the string of congressional hearings that have addressed television violence. Consider the five such congressional hearings held between 1988 and 1995. Of the 36 non-industry witnesses who testified against television violence, only seven were women. None was black or Hispanic. The 29 white males were identified as presidents, professors, directors, representatives, senators, senior scientists, and other distinguished titles that suggested they were well advanced in their careers. It is this patrician sector of society that for reasons of its own leads the attack on rowdy television violence.

The means by which one enters into society's dominant segment, and in doing so learns to affect reproachful views on television violence, is the academy. The general veneration that greets the academy is a sign of its near-sacred station and of the importance of its role in, as Bourdieu would view it, the reproduction of the dominant class and its habitus. Although the rewards of academics are middling in terms of financial capital, the cultural capital they accrue cannot be surpassed. To have a college degree—only about one-quarter of American adults do—is to have the credential of the dominant; not to have a college degree is to remain forever among the dominated.

Academics strive to regard television with condescension or an affected indifference. "A studied, conspicuous ignorance about television," communication professor Ellen Seiter wrote in 1996, "is a mark of distinction (like all distinctions, it is valued because it is so difficult to maintain)." Professors' general attitude toward television becomes more pointed when the topic of television violence is discussed; they are quick to assert piously that television is dangerously violent. Among college communication teachers, two-thirds of a 1991 sample of 486 instructors agreed that television "increased aggressive behavior." Of 68 scholars who had published papers or reports specifically on television's effects, 80 percent concurred that television violence produced aggressiveness.

Professors researching television's effects, therefore, seem to occupy a doubly honored position. Not only are they, like their colleagues, performing the crucial service of reproducing the dominant classes, but they also are breathing life into a key issue in the struggle between the dominant and the dominated. They may devote their entire careers to demonstrating the dangers of television violence and are bound to receive approbation from the dominant class as a result. No wonder the position of television effects researcher has proven so attractive.

Yet when a given skirmish over violence has exhausted itself and a lull sets in, members of the dominant class revert to their un-self-conscious viewing of televised mayhem. Even college professors watch TV. During one lull in the violence debate, a 1982 study found that media professors did not restrict their children's viewing any more than the rest of the population did.

Us vs. them

Perhaps the most striking conflict concealed in the debate over television violence involves the fabrication and control of "the Other." The best-known treatment of the concept of the Other is Edward Said's *Orientalism* (1978). The Orient, argued Said, was one of Europe's "deepest and most recurring images of the Other." It was "almost a European invention" that served as "a Western style for dominating, restructuring, and having authority over the Orient." Superiority over the Other was one motive for this phenomenon; another was self-definition. "The Orient," Said wrote, "has helped to define Europe (or the West) as its contrasting image, idea, personality, experience.

Thus the Other, the "not-us," is a fabrication used both to regulate those classified as the Other and to distinguish the culture of those doing the classifying. It is also a mechanism for emphasizing differences and disregarding similarities in order to maintain group solidarity. The Other differs conceptually from the mass in that the mass can be a part of "us," even if a discredited part, whereas the Other remains outside.

People do not worry about their own viewing of violent shows. . . . They worry extensively, however, about what the Dark Other is watching.

In the United States, the Other is often primarily a Dark Other—blacks and, to a lesser extent, Hispanics. The Dark Other is the recipient of an undeniable assault that plays out in racially charged terms. One form of the assault on the Dark Other is the War on Drugs. This "war" promotes definitions of legal and illegal drugs that have favored whites at the expense of the Dark Other; alcohol and prescription tranquilizers (both of whose records of extensive abuse and human damage are well documented) enjoy legal protection, whereas drugs associated with black culture, such as marijuana and cocaine (the health effects of which, on examination of the data, appear to be negligible), are proscribed. Of course, there is nothing inherent in these drugs that allocates them to the legal or illegal categories. These allocations are socially determined.

The anti-television violence crusades are part of this same assault. People do not worry about their own viewing of violent shows, and in fact they are so at peace with it that they are less likely to acknowledge the violence at all. They worry extensively, however, about what the Dark Other is watching. As British media scholar David Buckingham noted in 1997, "Debates about the negative effects of the media are almost always debates about other people."

"People like us" project a scenario onto the Dark Other in which viewing entertainment violence leads to real-life criminal behavior. This scenario is false in every detail—there exists no uniform Dark Other, and symbolic violence does not produce aggression—but it is upheld due to the emotional conviction behind it and the handy availability of ratio-nalizing "scientific proof." Fears of the Dark Other—fears of difference, of being preyed on, of having one's culture overturned, of invalidating one's identity—are denied expression elsewhere but are allowed to sneak into the attack on television violence. In this way, the Dark Other, his culture, his viewing habits, and his behaviors are disparaged.

There is a curious twist to all this, however—a complexity revealing much about the intricacies of social life. Whereas whites push off the Dark Other with vigor, at the same time they subtly beckon him back. Cultural theorists Peter Stallybrass and Allon White observe that whatever is excluded and displaced to the Other then becomes an object of fascination and is summoned back. The desire for cultural homogeneity produces instead a heterogeneous mix. Thus whites are fascinated by the music, dance, clothing styles, and behavior of blacks. Whites study black athletes, seeking to learn about the prowess of the Other. Whites welcome black entertainers, even when (or especially when) black actors are involved in violent scenarios.

Old vs. young

Adults who enlist in the anti-television crusade always insist that it is "impressionable youths" whom they wish to protect. In the guise of shielding youths, however, adults are trying to contain and control them.

This generational conflict emerges in contemporary polls: A 1997 survey by Steve Farkas and Jean Johnson of 2,000 randomly selected American adults found them ill disposed toward both younger children and adolescents. The majority of respondents used harsh terms to characterize 5-to-12-year olds, such as "lacking discipline," "rude," and "spoiled." Two-thirds of the respondents were very critical of teenagers, calling them "irresponsible" and "wild." According to the report, "Most Americans look at today's teenagers with misgiving and trepidation, viewing them as undisciplined, disrespectful, and unfriendly." Six hundred teenagers were also surveyed, however; they viewed things differently. Most felt happy in their lives and in their relationships with adults. These discrepant attitudes indicate much about the essential nature of generational strife—of who deprecates whom.

Age is the single most important factor in the viewing of television violence: Younger viewers watch much more than do older viewers.

Antagonism toward the young can be especially strong in an adult population configured like that of the United States—one that is aging rapidly due to the baby boom phenomenon. As subculture researcher Dick Hebdige observes, in the consciousness of adult society, "Youth is present only when its presence is a problem, or is regarded as a problem." Overall, adults feel threatened by the next generation.

Social scientist Charles Acland has argued that "youth's complex relationship with popular culture as a lived and expressive domain is menacing because the uses of culture cannot be policed completely." With adults able only partially to supervise the "menace" of popular culture, children and adolescents turn to their television shows, their movies, their computer games, and their music as an escape from adult restraint. Passing through a difficult stage in life, indeed perhaps the most strenuous one of all, youths turn to television violence for the vicarious release it can offer.

The consumption of symbolic violent content correlates negatively with age. According to a 1993 study commissioned by the Times Mirror Center for People and the Press, age is the single most significant factor in the viewing of television violence: Younger viewers watch much more than do older viewers. Cultural critic James Twitchell suggests that "if you study the eager consumers of vulgarities, you will soon see that this audience is characterized not so much by class (as we tend to assume, due in part to Marxist interpretations of the culture industry) as by maturity."

Youths do not think it probable that there could be any transfer from television's violence to aggression in the real world; of all age groups, they are the least likely to believe there is a connection. Elizabeth Kolbert, a *New York Times* reporter, interviewed three teenage felons on the subject in 1994 and noted, "The three teenagers . . . all scoffed at the notion that what young people see on the screen bore any relation to the crimes they committed."

Weaker vs. stronger

There are at least two cases where the anti-television crusade allows a weaker group to mount an attack against a stronger target. The first relates to the struggle between masculinity and femininity. As the male expresses dominion and the female resists it, everything in culture becomes gendered, or has reference to gender. This pervasive rivalry would be expected to find its way into the anti-television campaign as another camouflaged conflict between the dominant and the dominated, but in this instance the thrust is completely reversed. That is, when the struggle between genders enters into the debate over television violence, it does so as an act of resistance by the female against the male—as a small counterstrike.

The power of males is most pointedly realized in the violence some of them direct toward women.

Alert to the chance of male animosity, women are prone to feeling wary of violence even in its flattened, symbolic form on the television screen. The figment may draw too close to the real thing, whether experienced or imagined, to permit the degree of unimpeded pleasure that male viewers might enjoy. In surveys females are more likely than males to report there is "too much violence in television entertainment" and have been so since the general question was first asked in 1972. When queried about the amount of violence on specific action programs, women viewers will perceive more of it than will men, presumably because of their awareness of and uneasiness about the vicious content.

> *In surveys females are more likely than males to report there is "too much violence in television entertainment."*

The recurring moral crusade against television violence affords women a choice opportunity for retribution. Seemingly untainted by any overt hostility on its own part, the movement to purify televised entertainment, one that all agree is to be rhetorical only, seems to be shielded from any possibility of retaliatory strikes. How much contention against males is bound up in the 1994 assertion of Barbara Hattemer, president of the National Family Foundation, that "as media violence is absorbed into a person's thoughts, it activates related aggressive ideas and emotions that eventually lead to aggressive behavior"? How much gender strife is exposed in the hyperbolic 1996 statement of Carole Lieberman, chairperson of the National Coalition Against Television, that "more lives are damaged or destroyed by the effects of on-screen violence than by any other medical problem"? She has forgotten heart disease, cancer, and other maladies, and she has done so for a particular reason.

The religious right vs. the political left

The second case of a counterstrike against a stronger group involves religion. Many of the groups organized in opposition to television violence have religious ties. Here, neither the contestants nor their motives are camouflaged. The partisans on the attacking side are explicit and vociferous; they stand for religiosity, conservative beliefs, and "family values," and they are against licentiousness, media excesses, and symbolic violence. Those under attack—the entertainment industries and, by extension, all sorts of permissive people—respond first with incomprehension and then with annoyance, wishing the conservative and fundamentalist contingent would disappear. It would be easy for the political left to ignore the religious right if the latter did not comprise a well-defined and adamant voting bloc.

This cultural axis could hardly be more different from class antagonism. Social classes are stacked from bottom to top. Here, the axis and its poles can be understood as horizontal, stretching from the most conservative to the most free-thinking. Those gathered at the conservative and evangelical pole come from a wide range of social strata, although they are frequently depicted by their opponents as occupying lower-status positions exclusively. Seeking certainty in the literal word of the Bible, often believing in creationism and patriarchal traditions, and adhering to long-standing customs and attitudes, those clustered at this pole are often moved to take issue with the novelties of social transitions and the uncertainties of modern life.

Television violence allows conservative forces the opportunity to carry their standard forward.

Fundamentalists rail against the expanding, heaving tableau of television violence, and in organized fashion they strike out against it. The American Family Association (AFA), headed by the Rev. Donald Wildmon, has objected strenuously to video carnage. In 1993 Randall Murphree, editor of the association's *AFA Journal*, wrote: "Violence on the small screen continues to invade America's homes as television offers more graphic murders, bloodier assaults, and general mayhem. And all the while, the dramatic effects on society grow more and more alarming." In 1997 the AFA announced that, by its count, violent incidents in prime time network programs had increased 31 percent from the previous year—an increase far in excess of those measured by other monitors. As an example of the AFA's activities, in August 1997 its "Action Alert" roused its members to contact CBS and "express your concerns about their dangerous agenda of expanding the limits of violence on television through [the cop drama] *Brooklyn South."*

The issue of television violence affords groups such as the AFA the sanctioned opportunity to carry out a cultural attack—to have at their opponents, to condemn immoral depictions and the entertainment industry that produces and distributes them. Doing so, fundamentalism affirms its presence to others through an issue that is allowed to capture media attention and affirms its role to itself as a guardian of traditional mores. Television violence allows conservative forces the opportunity to carry their standard forward.

As religious conservatives react negatively to social changes of greater and lesser profundity, they may be performing an important service for American civilization. American culture is venturing into areas rarely if ever visited before, and never on such a large scale (for example, in matters of widespread individuality or of social inclusiveness). Some sort of conservative movement may prove useful, much like a sea anchor during turbulence, for steadying the vessel of culture.

The big lie

The widely held belief that television fantasy violence stimulates aggression in the real world and should be censured is what propaganda experts might call "a big lie"—a grotesque fabrication to which all unreflectingly subscribe. What makes this particular big lie different from the propagandists' is that it is not bestowed on an acquiescent population by some cabal; rather, this is one that we all repeatedly tell one another, duping ourselves as we dupe others. We do this for reasons of convenience: By repeating this uncontroverted big lie with ever-increasing volume, we can easily vent some of our own hostilities regarding other, truly confounding social conflicts.

While censure is generally directed by the stronger party toward the weaker, in some instances it flows in the opposite direction. Within the gender wars, and in the invectives of the religious right, condemnations are directed by weaker parties toward stronger targets. But whether the chastising energy flows from the stronger toward the weaker or from the weaker toward the stronger has nothing to do with the actualities of television violence.

The widely held belief that television fantasy violence stimulates aggression in the real world and should be censured is what propaganda experts might call "a big lie."

Whatever its immediate source, the energy that breathes life into the whipping boy of television violence has its ultimate origins in fear—fear of disorder that, in the extreme, could overturn society. As Charles Acland has written, "A society is always concerned with normalization, with the organization of its order, to assure the continuation of its structures and distribution of power." Although social order is a perpetual preoccupation, at this point in history it would seem to be an obsessive one; witness the outsized emphasis on the containment of crime at a time when crime is on the decline and the reckless hysteria of the War on Drugs. Sociologist Graham Murdock refers to the "fear about the precarious balance between anarchy and order in the modern age." Exactly why this fearful fixation on social order should be occurring now is open to question. Its existence, however, should not be doubted. Indeed, the need to strengthen social controls has a correlate in Americans' increasing imposition of self-controls: Per capita alcohol consumption and cigarette smoking have been on the decline and health club memberships on the rise for most of the past 30 years.

Television is new enough that it is not embraced without reservations, and it has not yet accumulated the social equity that would allow it to be shielded by nostalgia. In addition to its relative novelty, it is enormous, filling up the day (television viewing trails only work and sleep in terms of expended time), and can be menacing on this count. Because everyone has access to television, its use cannot be regulated, and thus for those who want to control it, the medium is believed to be out of control and threatening. The rise of television, observes media scholar Richard Sparks, "has been taken to signify the drift of history beyond willed control or direction. The censure of television bears witness to the fear of the future."

General apprehension about the course of history is in several senses the opposite of video violence—the passivity of fear vs. the frenzy of aggression, the amorphous vs. the detailed, and the actual vs. the symbolic. The two find each other as if magnetized, whereupon the flaying of the whipping boy begins.

6

Violence in the Movies Is a Serious Problem

Robert W. Butler

Robert W. Butler is a film critic for the Kansas City Star.

Popular movies are more violent now then ever before in the history of cinema. In Hollywood's first decades, bloodshed was hardly ever shown, but in the 1960s, filmmakers began showing more graphic depictions of violence with films like *Bonnie and Clyde* and *The Wild Bunch*. The 1980s saw the rise of the action-adventure film, with its high body counts, and in the 1990s films like *Pulp Fiction* played brutal violence for laughs. Violence has been so glamorized on the big screen that some viewers have been inspired to commit murder in the real world.

In the 1999 box office hit "The Matrix," Keanu Reeves dons a long black trench coat, picks up several rapid-fire weapons from a vast armory that seems to stretch to infinity, and wages war against the oppressive police who keep humanity in virtual slavery. He kills dozens of them.

And once again we find ourselves asking if the violence on our movie screens has bled over into real life.

We may never know if the movies contributed to the massacre at Columbine High School in Littleton, Colorado. Certainly the members of the "Trench Coat Mafia" were fashioning their own insular little world long before "The Matrix" opened.

What's undeniable is that in 1990s America, violent images are so commonplace as to be accepted as family entertainment, suitable for everyone from Grandma to wide-eyed preschoolers.

Movie violence has gone in 100 years from bloodless make-believe to graphic excess. What's usually missing from this cinematic world, though, is any examination of the wreckage violence leaves in its wake. Moviemakers have become experts at creating mayhem for the screen, even as they seem to have lost the ability or the will to confront its aftermath.

The early days of movie violence

Perhaps it began with Edwin S. Porter's 1903 silent "The Great Train Robbery," heralded as the birth of the narrative film in America. This Western featured several not-particularly violent deaths by gunfire; in a final coda that had unsophisticated audiences ducking for cover, a mustachioed cowboy aimed his pistol directly at the camera and pulled the trigger, filling the screen with smoke.

Even then, moviemakers realized that violence sold tickets.

There was violence on screen during the silent era, but its intensity was diluted by the relative primitiveness of the moviemaking process. The siege of Babylon sequence from D.W. Griffith's "Intolerance" has limbs and heads being struck off by swinging swords, but these moments are so obviously faked for the camera that they seem artificial, even quaint.

During Hollywood's Golden Era violent images on screen were strictly proscribed by the Motion Picture Production Code, a comprehensive list of do's and don'ts that all studio films were expected to conform to.

Violence was sanitized. Generations of boys grew up on the exploits of Roy Rogers, Gene Autry and other matinee idol cowboys whose blazing six-shooters rarely missed their targets but, curiously, never drew blood.

Bad guys fell dead without so much as a bullet hole in their black vests; when wounded, characters bore their discomfort stoically. There was no writhing in pain, no tears or screams of agony, no whimpering for one's mother, no mangled limbs—none of the real-life horrors that those little boys in the audience later encountered on the battlefields of World War II (and which were not realistically depicted until [1998's] "Saving Private Ryan," a rare war film that refused to glamorize combat).

Movie violence has gone in 100 years from bloodless make-believe to graphic excess.

The Production Code kept a lid on things. The idea was to entertain audiences, not upset them.

Even so, every now and then a director of conscience rubbed the fans' noses in it—as George Stevens did in the Western "Shane" (1953). The death of the farmer played by Elisha Cook Jr. at the hands of a professional killer (Jack Palance) was meant to shock. Cook was lifted off his feet by the bullet, flung backward and sent sliding across a muddy street as if shot from a cannon. Audiences had never seen anything like it.

This, the film seemed to say, is what violence is really like. It's ugly and ignominious, not neat and tidy like you've been led to believe.

The rise of graphic violence

The power of the Production Code eroded rapidly during the '50s and early '60s. The movie that rewrote the book on film violence was 1967's "Bonnie and Clyde."

On one level this landmark romanticized '30s bank robbers Bonnie Parker and Clyde Barrow (Faye Dunaway and Warren Beatty). But just when the audience got used to these protagonists as amusing rogues, the picture changed tone, producing one shocking scene of violence after another.

Audiences tend to remember Bonnie's and Clyde's deaths in a hail of machine gun fire, but the most shocking moment in the movie comes after the Barrow gang is ambushed at an Ozark cabin court. The criminals barely escape through a gauntlet of gunfire and take refuge in the woods. Clyde's brother Buck (Gene Hackman) collapses from a gaping head wound and lies on his back, shouting scrambled nonsense. His wife (Estelle Parsons) shrieks hysterically, her head wrapped in a towel bloody from the bullet wound that blinded her in one eye.

The movie that rewrote the book on film violence was 1967's "Bonnie and Clyde."

This was one of the first times in decades that American audiences had been allowed to see the aftermath of violence. It wasn't pretty.

A year later director Sam Peckinpah raised the ante with "The Wild Bunch," a Western punctuated with "blood ballets," brilliantly staged slow motion footage of men being struck by bullets. Peckinpah claimed he wanted to show the horror of violence, but in retrospect one wonders if he didn't make it seem almost too dreamlike, too beautiful.

In fact, with its armies of extras going down in graceful arcs of splattering gore, "The Wild Bunch" opened the door to what might be called "high-body-count" violence. Whereas earlier films had one or two bad guys whose elimination nicely wrapped up the drama, this new breed of film featured dozens—even hundreds—of on screen deaths.

The much-beloved "Star Wars" (1977) contributed to the trend. By encasing the bad guys—imperial storm troopers—in helmets that masked their features, director George Lucas allowed his good-guy protagonists to slay them with impunity. Storm troopers thus became less than human— they might as well be moving targets in an arcade shooting gallery.

In the '80s movie violence tended to combine the faceless enemy approach of "Star Wars" with ever more graphic special effects. In a score of movies Arnold Schwarzenegger, Sylvester Stallone and Bruce Willis mowed down entire armies of villains. These bullet-riddled losers could be Vietnamese soldiers, members of drug gangs, teams of gun-happy criminals . . . virtually any opponent deemed worthy of our contempt who could be painted in such broad strokes that audiences wouldn't think of them as human beings (which would, after all, take much of the fun out of it).

Not only were viewers invited to admire the creative ways in which these non-humans could be dispatched (bullets, explosions, stabbings, high-speed crashes), we were encouraged to applaud them, to laugh at the look of surprise on a drug gunman's face when he discovers our hero has the drop on him.

Audiences have become desensitized

In recent years an entirely new genre has appeared, one represented by "Pulp Fiction" and "Natural Born Killers" that views violence as a very black comedy. These films succeed in making us laugh at acts which should appall us.

It's easy to shrug all this off as little more than voyeuristic fantasy—until one considers the image of Eric Harris and Dylan Klebold moving deliberately through Columbine High, randomly shooting their fellow students. It is, of course, a scene that could have come from a high-body-count movie. To the shooters the victims weren't human—they were "jocks" or "heathers." Shoot one, make a wisecrack, laugh and move on to the next sucker.

Obviously everyone who watches film violence doesn't become a mass murderer. But it must be asked: Does screen violence so desensitize us that it paves the way for horrible events such as those that transpired in Littleton?

As residents of the 20th century we consider ourselves morally superior to the ancient Romans who made men and beasts fight to the death as public entertainment.

We've found our own way to enjoy that thrill: movie violence. And we think it's acceptable because nobody actually dies.

Perhaps it's time to ask just what dies in us when we watch it.

7

Violence in Video Games Is a Serious Problem

Eugene F. Provenzo Jr.

Eugene F. Provenzo Jr. is a professor of education at the University of Miami and the author of Children and Hyperreality: The Loss of the Real in Contemporary Childhood and Adolescence.

"First-person shooter" games such as Doom and Quake allow players to simulate the act of shooting people. The more people you can kill in these games, the better your score. These games effectively act as teaching machines that desensitize players to violence and make them better at killing. As computers become more sophisticated, the realism of these virtual-reality murder simulators will only increase.

Editor's note: The following remarks were presented to the Senate Committee on Commerce, Science, and Transportation at a March 21, 2000, hearing entitled "The Impact of Interactive Violence on Children."

My comments this morning must be brief. Much of what I will discuss is found in a new book I am working on entitled *Children and Hyperreality: The Loss of the Real in Contemporary Childhood and Adolescence*. It continues a line of inquiry I began in 1991 with *Video Kids: Making Sense of Nintendo*,[1] as well as in a number of articles and book chapters.[2] In this work, I am arguing that children and teenagers are spending much of their time in simulations, rather than in the natural or "real" world. It is an argument, which if true, has serious implications for not only our children, but also for the future of our society.

Essentially, I believe that the unreal, the simulation, the *simulacra* has been substituted for the real in the lives of our children. This occurs at many different levels: in the video games that are so much a part of the experience of contemporary childhood; in the shopping malls and "commercial civic spaces" where our children spend so much of their time; in television programs, advertisements and movies; in the theme parks

From Eugene F. Provenzo Jr.'s testimony before the Senate Committee on Commerce, Science, and Transportation on "The Impact of Interactive Violence on Children," March 21, 2000.

where we vacation; in the online chat rooms and discussion programs through which we communicate and exchange information; and finally, in the images of beauty and sexuality that run as a powerful undercurrent through much of our culture and the lives of our children.

As suggested above, the hyperrealities that increasingly shape and define the experience of childhood and adolescence come in many different shapes and forms. Some are clearly more detrimental than others.

Since this hearing focuses on "The Impact of Interactive Violence on Children," I will concentrate on what I consider to be the most disturbing aspect of my research—the increasing "romanticization" of violence—and more specifically, the frightening power and potential of the new video game technologies.

Let me begin by reflecting a bit on the information included on the recently released videotapes made by Eric Harris and Dylan Klebold shortly before the Columbine High School shootings in 1999.

It is very clear that Harris and Klebold wanted to tell the world a story whose script they seem to have learned through the entertainment media—particularly from ultra-violent films and video games. Harris tells his story in front of a video camera with a bottle of Jack Daniels and a sawed-off shotgun cradled in his lap. He calls the gun Arlene, after a favorite character in the *Doom* video game.

Harris and Klebold saw themselves as important media figures, whose story would be worthy of a filmmaker like Steven Spielberg or Quentin Tarintino. The fact that Harris and Klebold created these videotapes reminds me of the Mickey and Mallory characters in Oliver Stone's film *Natural Born Killers* who became media stars as a result of a murderous rampage across the country. It is no accident that the film was a favorite of Harris and Klebold.

I would like to argue that films and video games not only teach children about violence, but also how to be violent. When violence is stylized, romanticized and choreographed, it can be stunningly beautiful and seductive. At the same time, it encourages children and adolescents to assume a rhetorical stance that equates violence with style and personal empowerment.

Films and video games not only teach children about violence, but also how to be violent.

It does matter that we romanticize and stylize violence in films and video games.

It does matter that children and adolescents can put themselves into the virtual body of a killer in first-person shooter games.

It matters because a computer or video game is a teaching machine. Here is the logic: highly skilled players learn the lesson of game through practice. As a result, they learn the lesson of the machine and its software—and thus achieve a higher score. They are behaviorally reinforced as they play the game and thus they are being taught. Have you ever considered what it is they are being taught?

Consider first-person shooter games such as *Quake, Blood, Doom* or the recently released *Daikatana.* These are games that provide the player with a real-view perspective of the game. This is very different from the earlier tradition of video games like *Street Fighter II* or *Mortal Kombat,* in which the user viewed small, cartoon figures on the screen and then controlled their actions by manipulating them through a game controller. In contrast, a first-person shooter actually puts you inside the action of the game. The barrels of weapons like pistols and shotguns are placed at the bottom center edge of the computer screen. You can look right or left, up or down, by manipulating the computer mouse or game controller. The effect is one of literally stepping into the action of the game as a participant holding the weapon.

Lieutentant Colonel David Grossman, a former Professor of Psychology at West Point, argues that first-person shooter video games "are murder simulators which over time, teach a person how to look another person in the eye and snuff their life out."[3]

Dangerous games

Games like *Doom* are, in fact, used by military and police organizations to train people. The Marine Corps, for example, has adapted *Doom* to train soldiers in the Corps.

Some critics claim that there is little difference between what goes on in a first-person shooter and playing a game of Paintball, where players divide up on teams and hunt each other in a wood or elaborately constructed game room. To begin with, Paintball is acting that takes place in the real world. You run around a little, get tired and winded, bumped and scraped. There are serious consequences for getting out of control as you play—in other words—the fact that the game is physical and tangible means that it has limits. These limits not only include your own endurance, but the rules and procedures followed by your fellow players.

In a first-person shooter like *Quake* there are no boundaries or limits. The more "extreme" you are (a terminology often used in describing the action of the games), the more likely you are to win. Paul Keegan explains that in John Romero's recently released first-person shooter game *Daikatana:*

> Physical reality suggests that you are sitting in a chair operating a mouse and a keyboard. But with the computer screen replacing your field of vision, you believe you're actually creeping around a corner, causing your breath to shorten. Afraid an enemy is lying in wait, you feel your pulse quicken. When the monster jumps out, real adrenaline roars through your body. And few things in life are more exhilarating than spinning around and blowing the damn things to kingdom come, the flying gibs so lifelike you can almost feel wet blood.[4]

What is going on here is clearly different than just a game of Paintball or "Cowboys and Indians." However, the creators of first-person shooters just don't understand that there is a problem. John Carmack, the main creator of *Quake,* for example, considers the game nothing more than "playing Cowboys and Indians, except with visual effects."[5] In a recent interview, Carmack was reminded that in the past kids playing Cowboys and Indians weren't able to blow their brothers' heads off. His response was to laugh and say: "But you wished you could."[6]

Keep in mind this important fact: in first-person shooter games, players are not responsible for what they do. There are no consequences for other children, for families, or for society. As Mark Slouka explains in reference to the CD-ROM video game *Night Trap*, the game allows its players: "To inflict pain. Without responsibility. Without consequences. The punctured flesh will heal at the touch of a button, the scream disappear into cyberspace."[7]

Games that employ a first-person shooter model represent a significant step beyond the tiny cartoon figures that were included in *Mortal Kombat* in the mid-1990s. In fact, there has been a continuous evolution of the realism of these games as computing power has increased and become cheaper.

Much of this has to do with the enormous increase in computing power. A moderately fast desktop computer with a Pentium II chip that could be purchased for under $1,000 today has the speed of a $20 million Cray supercomputer from the mid-1980s.[8]

Even more interesting is the availability of inexpensive game consoles. Sony's dominance of this market has recently been challenged by Sega's amazing 200 Mhz Dreamcast game machine —available for nearly a year now in North America. It will soon be superseded by Microsoft's X-Box, which is designed specifically for interactive gaming, and which is set for release in the fall of 2001. The X-Box will be driven by a 600 Mhz Intel Pentium III chip. It will cost less than $500 and will allow players to go online to play games. The machine and the programs that will drive it represent what is potentially an extraordinary virtual reality simulator.

The creators of first-person shooters just don't understand that there is a problem.

Larry Smarr, director of the National Center for Supercomputer Applications in Champaign-Urbana, Illinois, believes that systems like these represent "the transition from people playing video games to a world where we will create our own fantasies in cyberspace."[9]

In many respects, the content of violent video games represents a giant social and educational experiment. Will these ultra violent games actually teach children to behave and view the world in markedly different ways? To repeat an earlier argument, video and computer games are, in fact, highly effective teaching machines. You learn the rules, play the game, get better at it, accumulate a higher score, and eventually win. As Mark Slouka argues, the implications of new technologies like video games "are social: the questions they pose, broadly ethical; the risks they entail, unprecedented. They are the cultural equivalent of genetic engineering, except that in this experiment, even more than the other one, *we* will be the potential new hybrids, the two-pound mice."[10]

It is very possible, that the people killed in the last few years as the result of "school shootings" may in fact be the first victims/results of this experiment. If this is indeed the case, it is an experiment *we* need to stop at once. Some things are too dangerous to experiment with.

Notes

1. Eugene F. Provenzo, Jr., *Video Kids: Making Sense of Nintendo* (Cambridge: Harvard University Press, 1991).

2. See: Eugene F. Provenzo, Jr., "'Brave New Video': Video Games and the Emergence of Interactive Television for Children," *Taboo: The Journal of Culture and Education,* Vol. 1, #1, Spring 1995, pp. 151–162; and Eugene F. Provenzo, Jr. "Video Games and the Emergence of Interactive Media for Children," in Shirley R. Steinberg and Joe L. Kincheloe, *Kinderculture: The Corporate Construction of Childhood* (Denver, Colorado: Westview Press, 1997), pp. 103–113.

3. Claymon, Deborah, "Video-game industry seeks to deflect blame for violence," *Miami Herald,* July 2, 1999, 3E.

4. Paul Keegan, "A Game Boy in the Cross Hairs," *The New York Times Magazine,* May 23, 1999, p. 38.

5. Ibid, p. 39.

6. Ibid.

7. Mark Slouka, *The War of the Worlds: Cyberspace and the High-Tech Assault on Reality* (New York: Basic Books, 1995), p. 13.

8. David E. Sanger, "High-Tech Exports Hit Antiquated Speed Bumps," *The New York Times,* June 13, 1999, WK 5.

9. John Markoff, "Silicon Valley's Awesome Look at New Sony Toy," *The New York Times,* March 19, 1999, p. C1.

10. Ibid.

The Problem of Video Game
Violence Is Exaggerated

Greg Costikyan

*Greg Costikyan is a game designer currently with Unplugged Games. He
also writes frequently about gaming and is the author of four novels.*

Violence is a prominent theme in video games, and some games
have depicted violence in crude and ugly ways. But in the majority of cases violence is only part of a game's appeal. The first-
person shooter games that do center around violence actually
benefit society because they give young males a way to vent their
antisocial impulses without harming anyone. The outcry against
violent video games is reminiscent of past panics over comic
books, rock music, and role-playing games. All these attacks on
youth culture have had little justification in reality.

About 10 years ago, I had drinks with Frank Chadwick, then president
of a game publisher called Game Designers Workshop. At the time,
the Game Manufacturers Association was trying to reposition hobby
games as "adventure games"—which we both thought risible.

Chadwick said, "You know, a better name for our industry would be
'violence gaming.'"

I flinched, of course. But Chadwick had a point: hobby games then
consisted mainly of war games—war is certainly violent—and role-
playing games, whose players spend much of their time in combat against
fantastic monsters or comic-book supervillains and such.

Violence is intrinsic to many, many games. Even as abstract a game
as chess can be seen as a form of military conflict.

When I was a kid, "gaming" meant the mass-market boardgame industry and a small hobby-game appendage that together grossed perhaps
a few hundred million dollars at retail. Today, it includes computer, con-
sole and arcade gaming and is a $7 billion industry in the U.S. alone—
the second largest entertainment industry in the world, after film and
television.

As McLuhan would have it, every medium has a message. If violence

From "Games Don't Kill People—Do They?" by Greg Costikyan. This article first appeared in
Salon.com, at www.Salon.com. An on-line version remains in the Salon archives. Reprinted with
permission.

is intrinsic to gaming, and if gaming is an increasingly predominant form of entertainment, is the likely consequence to our society an increase in violence?

Is video game violence a problem?

Are the critics who attack gaming in the wake of the Littleton massacre correct on the fundamentals? Should Congress ask the surgeon general to prepare a report on how video games spur youth violence, as it is considering? Do games stoke our violent instincts—or sublimate them? Is there such a thing as "good violence" and "bad violence" in games?

Let's step back a moment. What *is* a game?

A game is an interactive structure that requires players to struggle toward a goal.

If there's no interaction, it isn't a game; it's a puzzle. If there's no goal, then the players have no reason to choose one option over another, to undertake one task instead of something else; there's no structure. If achieving the goal isn't a struggle, if winning is easy, the game is dull; winning's no thrill.

Struggle implies conflict. Just as conflict is at the core of every story, conflict is at the core of every game. That doesn't mean all conflict must be violent; in a story, the central conflict can be the protagonist's own feelings of inadequacy, or the obduracy of her in-laws, or the inequities of society. But violent conflict has its uses; otherwise, we wouldn't have horror stories and mysteries and thrillers. Not to mention "Hamlet" and "Henry V."

There are as many ways to create conflict in a game as in a story. Adventure games like Myst use puzzles. Games like Diplomacy require negotiation. Builder games like Civilization require you to overcome economic and technological obstacles.

But there's no way to avoid conflict entirely. No conflict, no struggle. No struggle, no obstacles. No obstacles, no work. No work, no fun.

The appeal of Quake

Where does violence come into the picture? Violence is an easy out. It's the simplest, most obvious way to make a game a struggle. If achieving your goal requires you to get through a horde of ravenous, flesh-eating monsters, the conflict is clear—and the way to win is equally clear. You kill them.

Obstacles-of-violence, to coin a term, are compelling; the kill-or-be-killed instinct is wired into our hind-brain, part of our vertebrate heritage. Games like Quake II trigger a visceral, edge-of-the-seat response. Precisely because you can be killed at any moment by strange and nasty creatures, because only quick reactions can defeat them, Quake is a compelling experience.

Quake uses violence well. By that, I mean that it achieves precisely the effect its designers wished to achieve, and succeeds in delivering a compelling, stimulating, entertaining, intense experience to the player. It is a fine game.

But still: Violence is not the *only* way to achieve struggle in games. It is merely the easiest, the simplest, the most obvious tool in the game designer's armamentarium.

So—are games fundamentally violent and therefore bad? No. Chadwick was wrong; games are not *about* violence. Games are about struggle. Because violence is the easiest way to create struggle, many games are violent—but far from all.

But perhaps a more sophisticated argument still holds water? Perhaps game designers have insouciantly awoken the beast, cavalierly creating entertainment so violently compelling that it teaches violence, desensitizes us, spurs increased violence in our society?

[Violence is] the simplest, most obvious way to make a game a struggle.

There *is* a lot of violence in computer gaming. Some of it is very ugly. The two most popular categories in computer games at present are the first-person shooter (Quake, Unreal, Half-Life) and the real-time strategy game (StarCraft, Myth, Total Annihilation). Both categories are "games of violence," if you will.

The computer gaming industry is a monoculture. It consists almost entirely of white, suburban males in their 20s. We're talking the demographic that reads *Maxim* magazine. They're heavily into computer games, almost completely ignorant of games from other media and almost equally ignorant of computer games published longer than five years ago. Visiting a game development firm is like walking into a strangely 1950s version of 1990s America; if any women are on the premises, they're artists or marketing people. You may see some Asians, you might see a programmer from India, but certainly nobody darker.

Unsavory excess

Developers play the same games, they see the same movies, they fraternize with people like themselves and they develop some pretty weird mind sets. Violence is perceived as cool—no, not real violence, but violence in games.

Consider Postal, published two years ago. It's a shooter in which you play a deranged, psychotic loser. You wander around shooting completely innocent people at random.

It's hard to imagine why anyone thought this was a good idea. For one thing, innocent people do not make good obstacles: They're unlikely to shoot back. They're not particularly threatening. Never mind the moral considerations; this makes for a dull game.

And the moral considerations should certainly have made Postal's developers (a company called Running with Scissors) think twice. No doubt, they assumed that the "edgy" nature of the project would get them a lot of press and boost its sales. They did get a lot of press, almost all of it negative, and no doubt that did spur some sales to the kind of people who actually think "Beavis & Butthead" is funny.

But you know what? Postal failed. It didn't achieve anywhere near expected sales. The reviews were almost uniformly negative. It failed because it was a bad game.

Consider the "bathtub of blood" ad (for the game Blood, developed by Monolith for GT Interactive). It ran in computer gaming magazines in 1997 (for example, the front gatefold of *Computer Gaming World,* May 97). The dominant image of the advertisement was, literally, a bathtub filled with blood.

It's hard to imagine why *anyone* thought this was effective advertising. What it said was: Our game is violent. Our sense of humor is crass. It didn't actually do what an advertisement *must* do—explain why the product will be fun or useful, establish a compelling value proposition for the consumer.

Only computer game developers could ever have thought this was a good idea.

In March, another advertisement, for an online games retailer, appeared in the computer gaming press (for instance, *Computer Gaming World,* March 99, page 89). Its dominant image is that of the naked torso of a woman, lying on an operating table, the rest of her body outside the frame. In the foreground are surgically-gloved hands, holding a scalpel. In the woman's bare flesh are incised the lines of a tic-tac-toe game.

I buy a lot of computer games. I generally buy them online. But the image of someone cutting a woman's flesh in order to play the most patently brain-dead game imaginable did not make me want to patronize this company's services. God only knows why they thought it would motivate anyone else.

Certainly, it is an arresting image. Arresting enough to make the gorge rise. Only the computer gaming culture could possibly view any of this as effective, appropriate or funny.

So perhaps the critics are correct, at least to this degree: The coolness of violence, as portrayed in computer games, has persuaded computer game developers, if no one else, that nauseating depictions of violence, whether or not effective, are cool.

In the gaming field, the response to post-Littleton attacks has been self-righteously defensive. It's just a game. It doesn't hurt you any more than TV (never mind the damage television has done to our political system, our propensity to read, and our sense of social solidarity). Games Are Cool.

That's understandable. Computer gaming people have virtually no defense *other* than self-righteousness. They're guilty of many of the sins ascribed to them.

But consider this: The excesses fail. Postal failed. Those ads do not deliver. Violence alone doesn't do the trick. Violence is, and should be, part of a designer's toolkit; but it is neither necessary nor sufficient.

Artistic violence

Every year, Brian Moriarty gives a speech at the Game Developers Conference, one of the industry's main trade shows. Every year, it is the best-received speech at the conference. Moriarty is a brilliant speaker, but more than that, he is one of the industry's *eminences grises*—one of the original Infocom crew, creator of Loom and Beyond Zork, now in charge of development at MPlayer (one of the biggest of the online-game communities).

Last year, Moriarty's speech was on the subject of violence in games. As he spoke, two short clips appeared on a screen behind him, repeating hypnotically. One was a clip from "The Great Train Robbery," a silent film historians call the first real movie hit, showing a mustachioed Westerner shooting a gun directly toward the camera; the other, a short sequence from Quake, showed a guard being shot.

Compelling images both—and compelling in that both show that violence has been a important part of two very different media, virtually from their inceptions.

There is a lot of violence in computer gaming. Some of it is very ugly.

The speech itself was a meditation on two issues: first, the nature of violence in gaming; and second, the idea of "rhythm of play." Moriarty says that, if you observe people playing a game—observe them, not the game itself—you find that they engage in repeated cycles of activity. And this repetition, the rhythm created, is one of the strongest draws for people to interactive entertainment. It's hypnotic. It's involving.

Violence, he says, creates dissonance. It breaks the rhythm. Dissonance is not bad in itself; dissonance, consciously and creatively used, can be an extremely effective technique, in gaming as in music.

"If you want to include violence in your games," says Moriarty, "do it, and put your heart and soul into it, do it with awareness—not because violence is easy, or because it shocks, but because you need dissonance, and you know how and why it strengthens your game."

To paraphrase: Violence used artistically is effective; violence used crudely is vile.

It's a lesson most computer-game developers have yet to learn—and if one of the upshots of Littleton is that they begin to think more clearly about the issue, that will be to the good.

The hysteria over first-person shooters

First-person shooters are violent games. Yet they are not depictions of endless, orgasmic mayhem; in their solo-play mode, they are mainly about exploration and puzzle-solving, with opposition provided in the form of monsters you shoot. Though violence, and the edge-of-the-seat tension it builds, is a key part of the game's aesthetic, impressive 3D technology and art and clever "level design" (where exploration and puzzle-solving come in) are at least as important.

The "violence" is against monsters, defined as such, who are clearly attempting to kill you; the back story, such as it is, presents them as some kind of horrible, Lovecraftian intrusion into the real world. Hence they are, in a sense, totally depersonalized opponents. But the notion that this kind of thing therefore "desensitizes" people to violence and makes them more willing to commit it seems dubious. Shooters are really about the "booga-booga" fright instinct: A scary monster appears out of nowhere and roars at you; you have to turn quickly and blow it away.

And of course, you die frequently yourself. The feeling engendered is not "I'm an immortal Rambo, I'm so cool I can kill anything"—rather, it's more like, "God, that was a hard level, those spider things with the cannon launchers are really tough, I'm glad I finally got through it."

Interestingly, the multiplayer online version is very different. You shoot not monsters but other players, who are running around trying to kill you. And they aren't depersonalized; they look just like you, you can chat with them (but rarely do because the game is too fast-paced), and so forth. This has been portrayed as something new and frightening—but frankly, it's no different from paintball and not much different from tag.

Violence used artistically is effective; violence used crudely is vile.

The press has reported Lt. Col. David Grossman's claim that games like Quake are good training for murder, because they teach you to "clear a room" by moving quickly from target to target and aiming for the head. They teach you to avoid the novice hunter or soldier's mistake of shooting repeatedly at the same target until the target drops, and instead to use only a single shot.

On the basis of this, I have to doubt that Grossman has ever actually played Quake. No monster in Quake can be killed with a single shot; at least two hits are required. It is impossible to make a "head-shot"; Quake makes no distinction between shots that strike at different locations on a target's body. And if you stay still long enough to pick your targets and get off head-shots, you're dead. You must keep moving to evade enemy fire. You snap off shots when you can.

In short, Quake doesn't teach the lessons that the critics claim it teaches.

The development of shooting games over time has not been toward more and more megaviolence; rather, it's been toward prettier and more-impressive 3D rendering (Unreal) and toward more compelling story-lines, interwoven more effectively with the game (Half-Life).

Yes, these are violent games—but as is usually the case when the media latches onto something, they have been caricatured. Violence is only a part of their appeal.

Part of human nature

The idea that film or television or books make people violent has been debunked again and again. (For one thing, if it were true, Japan would, judging by its popular culture, surely be filled with violent pederasts instead of the civilized world's most peaceful and orderly population.)

But perhaps computer games are different—so uniquely compelling that violence in games does breed violent behavior?

Some 25 years ago, I read through the Whole Earth Catalog. One section of the book was devoted to the war games published by Simulations Publications Inc.—and I was then an avid war gamer (and later employed by that company) so I, naturally, read it carefully. The Whole Earth Catalog was written during the Vietnam War, a period when schools shied away from any discussion of warfare or military history as too hot a topic to consider. But, as the publication said, war has been part of human nature since time immemorial. War is worthy of study, if only so that we can avoid it by understanding it more fully. And, perhaps, war games are our best hope of avoiding future wars. Perhaps the things we find attractive about war, perhaps the impulses that lead us to war, can be satisfied through simulation.

Violence, and the attraction of violence, is a fundamental part of human nature. It is particularly appealing to young adolescent males, for it is a clean break with the rules-bound environment in which they have lived, a rejection of parental order. In every society, violence is most common among young men.

It is foolish to try to change human nature; it is immutable, or mutable only through the slow process of evolution. What can be changed is society. Society can develop institutions and mechanisms to channel antisocial impulses to pro-social purposes. That's one reason for armies, of course; they institutionalize violence in a mechanism designed to protect rather than damage society.

The benefits of violent video games

And games of violence? They allow players to *be* violent, to act out their violent impulses, to hunt and shoot and kill—in a way that harms no one.

Listen to the boastfulness of Quake players on TEN. They'll kill your pussy ass. They'll blow you up so good your spleen will land in Chicago and your liver in Des Moines. They're profane and obnoxious, and violently so.

They're blowing up pixels. They're killing bitmaps. They're shooting at software subroutines.

They're not a threat to public order, for chrissakes. What they're doing makes them less likely to be a threat to public order. They're getting their jones—they're satisfying their antisocial impulses in a completely harmless way.

Violent computer games don't spur violence; violent computer games channel antisocial impulses in societally acceptable ways.

Games are good.

The same old argument

For those of us who've been involved in gaming for a long time, the whole hysteria over Littleton brings forth a strong sense of *deja vu*.

We've been through this before. Fifteen years ago, Dungeons & Dragons was the culprit. Every time some kid killed himself and a copy of D&D was found amid the stuff in his room, the papers would run a story about how those vile fantasy role-playing games made him do it. The fundamentalists latched onto it, too; Dungeons & Dragons involved magic and spells, and to fundamentalists of a certain stripe, that means it must be inherently demonic and evil.

Poor Sandy Petersen is the man I sympathized with most. He designed Call of Cthulhu, a role-playing game based on the horror stories of H.P. Lovecraft. He's a devout Mormon. His game was repeatedly attacked, and he along with it, as one of the most demonic and evil of the lot: After all, it deals explicitly with demons from other dimensions. He found himself on panels at gaming conventions, trying to explain to gamers that all Christians were not vile, censoring, irrational scum—and I have no doubt he found himself trying to explain to his co-religionists why all gamers weren't evil Satanic monsters.

The development of shooting games over time has not been toward more and more megaviolence.

If I feel a sense of *deja vu*, how much worse it must be for him. Sandy co-designed Doom II and Quake.

It's not just Dungeons & Dragons. We went through this when the Internet first came to prominence, and was blamed for sex crimes and pederasty. We went through it in the '50s, when comic books were attacked as perverting our youth, leading to the death of EC Comics and the establishment of the Comics Code Authority. We went through it in the '30s, when LaGuardia took his hatchet to pinball machines across New York.

Hell, we went through it with rock 'n' roll.

Young people are the ones most open to novelty. Consequently, they lead the way in the adoption of any new entertainment medium. Parent/teenager relationships being what they are, parents invariably view the new medium as threatening. The nature of our journalism-industrial complex being what it is, some pundits seize on the fear as a means of achieving an audience. The most threatening aspects of the medium are puffed up into a major threat to civilization. Kids find their medium under attack, and respond, naturally, by embracing the aspects under attack most wholeheartedly.

Sometimes, as with Dungeons & Dragons, the attack ultimately dissipates under the weight of its own ludicrous contradictions. Sometimes, as with EC Comics, congressional hearings and an abject surrender by the industry result.

Give the games a chance

But these attacks, all of them, have nothing to do with reality. They're about fear. They're about the fear of the new—the fear of parents who see their children doing something they don't understand and worry about the consequences.

The attack is an argument from ignorance. It has no rational basis. It is made by people who don't understand what they attack, and find its indicia frightening. And to the degree that they have any credibility at all, it's because ugly and repulsive violence *does* exist within computer gaming. And if the industry has the brains God gave a biscuit, it will respond—not by imposing censorship or another inane rating scheme, but by avoiding the kind of repulsive, exploitative violence that any idiot ought to see is not going to work anyway.

If *you* are concerned about violence in gaming, I have one piece of advice: Go buy a copy of Quake II. Install it on your machine. Download a walkthrough, so you won't fear humiliation when you play. And give it a try.

I think you'll find that it's not so frightening. You may even have a good time.

You might even find yourself—like me—shopping for a home networking kit and running cable, so you can play games with your kids.

9

The Glamorization of Guns in Rap Music Is a Serious Problem

Jay Nordlinger

Jay Nordlinger is managing editor of the National Review, *a conservative weekly magazine.*

Many so-called "gangsta" rappers make a living selling albums that glorify guns and violence. Some of the most successful of these rappers practice what they preach: The rapper Notorious B.I.G. was shot to death in 1997, and Sean "Puffy" Combs was arrested for illegal weapon possession following a shooting at a nightclub in 1999. Anti-gun activists have not spoken out about these incidents or the role of guns in hip-hop culture because they do not want to alienate blacks. But there is no denying that gangsta rap's fixation on gun violence harms society.

A lot of people were interested in the Sean "Puffy" Combs trial: fans of rap music; celebrity-watchers; connoisseurs of popular culture. But one group of people showed no interest whatsoever: gun-control activists. This was rather strange—a dog that didn't bark. The Combs case was awash in guns; so is Combs's world—that of rap, or "hip-hop." But the gun-controllers prefer to ignore this dark corner. Their indifference, or passivity, may be taken to represent a broader failure of liberalism to confront ghetto culture—to look it in the eye and cry, "No!"

Combs—known as "Puff Daddy"—is a major figure in rap, the boss of a record label called "Bad Boy." (Another label is called "Murder, Inc."—one refreshing thing about the rappers is their lack of pretense.) The Combs case dominated New York at the beginning of 2001, the trial of a century that is still very young. What happened is this: In December 1999, Combs visited a nightclub with his girlfriend (the pop star Jennifer Lopez), a few "associates," and several of his guns. Someone insulted Combs. Shooting broke out. Three people were injured, two of them badly. Then Combs and his group fled the scene. When the police finally caught up with the getaway car—or rather, the getaway Lincoln Navigator SUV—they found two guns. Combs was subsequently charged with illegal weapons possession and bribery (he had tried to get his driver to accept responsibility for the guns). The rapper's guilt seemed clear, but he denied everything.

In a now-de rigueur move, Combs hired Johnnie Cochran, the O.J. Simpson lawyer, who composed a few new rhymes and flashed his smile at the jury. Combs got off. One of those "associates," however, was not so lucky: Jamal "Shyne" Barrow—a rapper described as Combs's protege—was found guilty of first-degree assault. He now faces 25 years in prison.

"Gangsta" rappers . . . glory in guns and gun violence in song after song after song.

So, another day, another rap case—this time, no one died. It's easy to look away from rap and its nature. But it should not be so, and it certainly shouldn't be so for gun-controllers. Thug rappers should be their worst nightmare (and a lot of other people's). Yet the anti-gun activists would rather go after Charlton Heston [president of the National Rifle Association], rednecks, and other soft targets. It's far more comfortable to torment the NRA, which advocates not only gun rights but gun safety, than to get in the faces of "gangsta" rappers, who glory in guns and gun violence in song after song after song. Most people, by now, are familiar with rap's hideous and constant degradation of women (where are the feminists, incidentally?). They are less familiar with rap's celebration of the gun. Back in 1992, there was a brief furor over a rap called "Cop Killer." The idea of gunning down policemen is certainly an attention-getter. But if rappers are enthusing only about killing one another, that seems to be another matter, something to be swept under the rug.

Liberals have occasionally been interested in this subject. Tipper and Al Gore were, before Hollywood bit their heads off. Usually, though, when you try to interest liberals in the horrors of today's worst music, they roll their eyes and recall how their parents railed against "Elvis's pelvis." Ah, the two magic words: "Elvis's pelvis." Say them, and you shut down any discussion about, for example, rap's effects on the young. And doesn't every generation murmur, with a sigh and a shake of the head, "Kids today . . ."? But any sensate being can see that "gangsta" rap—with its sanction, even urging, of rape, murder, and other abuse—has nothing at all in common with Elvis Presley's swaying hips. It must be, in part, a fear of uncoolness—of fogeydom—that keeps many people from coming to grips with rap. They are perfectly happy to claim that the sight of Joe Camel causes millions of young'uns to smoke cigarettes; but they are reluctant to consider what rap—poured constantly into young ears—might do.

The object of their affections

Rappers sing of guns with almost lascivious glee. They express close to an erotic feeling about their "pieces": "glocks" (for the Austrian manufacturer), "gats" (short for Gatlings), "nines" or "ninas" (for 9mm pistols), and so on in a long and chilling lexicon. Bullets and clips are lingered over as eyes and lips might be in love songs. Here's a sample from "Trigga Gots No Heart" by the rapper Spice 1: "Caps [bullets] peel from gangsters in my 'hood. You better use that nina 'cause that deuce-deuce [.22-caliber weapon] ain't no good, and I'm taking up a hobby, maniac murderin', doin' massacre robbery." There is no end of material like this. The rapper Notorious B.I.G., slain by gun in 1997, sang, "Somebody's gotta die. Let the gunshots blow. Somebody's gotta die. Nobody gotta know that I killed yo' a** in the midst, kid." And, "Don't fill them clips too high. Give them bullets room to breathe. Damn, where was I?" Dr. Dre had a hit called "Rat-Tat-Tat-Tat," whose refrain went, "Never hesitate to put a nigga on his back. Rat-tat-tat-tat to the tat like that, and I never hesitate to put a nigga on his back."

During the Combs trial, some thought that Shyne Barrow's lyrics would do the young man no good. They are horrible, but since millions of kids drink them in, their parents might as well know them, too. In "Bad Boyz," Barrow raps, "Now tell me, who wanna f*** with us? Ashes to ashes, dust to dust. I bang and let your f***in' brains hang . . . My point is double-fours [a .44 magnum] at your f***in' jaws, pointed hollow point sh** [this is bullet terminology], four point six [?], need I say more? Or do you get the point, b**ch?" In another track—"Bang"—he says, "Niggas wanna bang. We could bang out till the clip's done, or your vital arteries hang out." And: "Got my mind right, like Al Pacino and Nino. I head to Capitol Hill to kidnap Janet Reno. Words droppin' and shockin', guns cockin' and poppin', somebody call Cochran" (that would be the lawyer Johnnie—life imitating art, or is it the other way around?). Barrow continues, "No time to waste, nine in my waist, ready for war, any time, any place. F*** it, just another case."

Rappers sing of guns with almost lascivious glee.

Are these words meant to be taken seriously, or are they just play—disturbing, maybe, but basically harmless? Shyne Barrow did, indeed, have a "nine in his waist" at that nightclub, and it appears to have been luck that he didn't kill the people he hit. Moral relativism, however, is rife in discussion about rap (such as it is). Barrow's lawyer, Murray Richman, made the following, delicious comment to the *New York Post* last December [2000]: "Dostoyevsky wrote about murder—does that implicate him as a murderer?" Or "when Eartha Kitt salaciously sings 'Santa, Baby,' does that mean she really wants to sleep with Santa Claus?" This sort of statement is meant to be a conversation-stopper, like "Elvis's pelvis." You know: Dostoyevsky, Eartha Kitt, Shyne Barrow—artists all, and liable to be misunderstood by the conservative and hung-up. "Kids today . . ."—ha ha.

Gun control and gangsta rap

Now, gun-control groups are concerned—and why shouldn't they be?—with laws and loopholes and gun shows and accidents in homes and Charlton Heston and, of course, school shootings, out of which they make hay. They say nothing about hip-hop culture, and next to nothing about popular culture generally. The groups put out a steady stream of press releases: praising states' "safety initiatives," trying to shame manufacturers, worrying about "children's health." In fact, they seem to burrow into every nook and cranny of American life—but keep mum about the ghetto and its anthems.

Nancy Hwa is spokesman for Handgun Control, Inc. (the Jim and Sarah Brady group). She says that her organization has "called on people in the creative industry not to glamorize guns," but has not dealt with hip-hop in particular. "Other targets have a more direct relationship with getting your hands on guns," she says—for example, "sales at gun shows." And no one group, she sensibly points out, can cover everything. Plus, "when it comes right down to it, you can listen to rap or Marilyn Manson or country music, and, in the end, as long as the young person can't get their hands on a gun, all they're guilty of is questionable taste in music." For Handgun Control, Inc., the issue is "access," plain and simple.

There should be no disagreement about the awfulness—why not go all the way? the evil—of the most violent, dehumanizing, and desensitizing rap.

Ted Pascoe speaks for Do It for the Kids!, a gun-control group in Colorado. "We don't address it," he says of the rap issue. "We have enough trouble with the Second Amendment without attacking the First as well." Meaning? "Well, there is a perception in this country that individuals enjoy the protections conferred by the Second Amendment. But that amendment only confers on states the right to maintain militias. So the individual has no standing in court to make Second Amendment claims. However, Americans tend to believe they do have the right to bear arms. So, it's troublesome, because whenever you start talking about passing stronger gun laws, a lot of folks—even if they're not involved in the issue, or vested in it—can invoke the Second Amendment and sometimes effectively take the wind out of your sails." A stance against rap, says Pascoe, would only bring trouble: "The large number of gun-control groups don't want to be seen as attacking every element in the Constitution, or more than one. I think that the First Amendment contains rights that we do enjoy—that individuals have First Amendment rights."

The confusion of rights and responsibilities—of "what you got a right to do and what is right to do," as the supreme fogey Bill Bennett puts it—is an old one.

Andy Pelosi, who represents New Yorkers Against Gun Violence, says that his group "really focuses on legislative issues—we've done a little bit of violence in the media, but not rap." He makes the point that "it would be unfair to look at one genre without looking at the others. You could make a case about heavy metal, alternative rock—you wouldn't want to single out just rap." This would, indeed, be a painful step for most liberals. It would involve a clash of their pieties: gun control—outright demonization of the gun—and a taboo against taking issue with black culture in any of its aspects. The old "No enemies to the left" might mingle with a new slogan: "No enemies among blacks" (with Clarence Thomas and the other Toms excepted, of course).

Speaking out against hate rap

The country is engaged in a great debate over gun control; but there should be no disagreement about the awfulness—why not go all the way? the evil—of the most violent, dehumanizing, and desensitizing rap. The inner city is bleeding from gun crime. White America should probably think harder about the perpetual Columbines taking place in ghettos. Of course, many excuse rap on grounds that it merely reflects life on the mean streets. And whether this stuff has bloody consequences is an open question. In 1993, a rapper called Masta Ace, talking to the *St. Petersburg Times,* said, "It's like a Schwarzenegger movie—you don't come out wanting to shoot anybody." But he quickly had a second thought: "I think it does shape mentalities and helps develop a callousness to where you could really shoot somebody and not think twice about it."

Sure: There's only so much a gun-control group or conservative alarm-raisers or anyone else can do about (what might be termed) hate rap. But activists, who love to talk—it is their principal activity—might at least talk. A group called the Campus Alliance to End Gun Violence proclaims as its number-one position, "Gun violence disproportionately preys on the young. Silence kills. We must speak." Well, all right: Minus a right-wing militia or two, there is only one class of people—an extremely wealthy and popular class of people—that actually exalts gun violence. So . . . ?

10

The Problem of Violent Themes in Popular Music Is Exaggerated

Hillary B. Rosen

Hillary B. Rosen is the president and chief executive officer of the Recording Industry Association of America.

A 2000 report by the Federal Trade Commission expressed concern over the marketing of violent entertainment, including music with violent or sexually explicit lyrics, to youth. In response the Recording Industry Association of America has tightened its already strong guidelines regarding advertising and the use of parental advisory labels on records, tapes, and CDs. However, those concerned about violent lyrics in music should remember that there is no evidence linking music with violent behavior. Indeed, violent crime fell in the 1990s even as music sales increased. Finally, violence is a recurring theme in many types of music, including opera and country, so rap should not be singled out for its violent lyrics.

Editor's note: The following remarks were presented to the Senate Committee on Commerce, Science, and Transportation at a September 13, 2000, hearing on the marketing of violent entertainment to youth.

I am President and CEO of the Recording Industry Association of America. RIAA is the trade association of America's record companies. Our membership is as diverse as our music.

I speak for thousands upon thousands of people in the recording industry. Our views on youth violence and culture—just like those of members of this committee and others who testify before it—are not informed by their professional capacities alone.

They are informed by our dreams for our own kids—our concerns about our community—and our commitment to our country.

From Hillary B. Rosen's statement before the Senate Committee on Commerce, Science, and Transportation, September 13, 2000.

We are proud to be members of an industry who work with artists to create the most diverse music in the world filled with a multitude of musical styles, lyrical imagination and cultural experiences. And we are also proud of our 15-year track record of helping parents make informed choices about their children's entertainment.

Throughout that period, the issue of how entertainment affects children has wandered back and forth between the headlines from the back pages. But we have been consistent.

Today, as the issue finds itself back on the front pages again, we are proud to speak with you just as authoritatively and every bit as passionately as we have for each of the last 15 years.

Today, Mr. Chairman, I want to explain how the recording industry's system works, how it has been improved and attempt to specifically address some of the FTC's criticisms.

In an average retail store with 110,000 titles, about 500 will carry the Parental Advisory logo. That's less than one-half of one percent.

I am somewhat hampered in the latter task. The public or members of this Committee may not realize this but while some (including this Committee's staff) were apparently briefed on the report a few weeks ago Mr. Chairman, we only received it two days ago. The FTC had over one year to do all of its analysis, compile a hundred page report and a 250 or so page annex with thousand of footnotes containing significant detail and assumptions and we have had 48 hours to look at it before this hearing.

The recording industry's voluntary program

The premise of our system is to balance an artist's right of self-expression with a parents' need for information to make choices based on their children's individual situation and their own values.

In 1985, we reached agreement on that approach with the National Parent Teacher Association and the Parents Music Resource Center. Within months, music releases with explicit lyrics, whether about violence or sex, were identified.

I should add that despite the emphasis at these hearings on recordings with explicit content, they comprise a relatively small proportion of our industry's output and the themes and language contained in all of our music is a part of today's society.

In an average retail store with 110,000 titles, about 500 will carry the Parental Advisory logo. That's less than one-half of one percent of that store's total inventory. And the major labels produce clean versions of nearly all recordings that carry the logo.

And let me assure you, Mr. Chairman, that this industry is a very tough customer. Recently a story in the *New York Times* carried this headline: "Recording Industry's Strictest Censor Is Itself."

Is this system perfect? Of course not. Even if it had been, entertainment is a constantly evolving industry.

So where our system was imperfect, we have tried to improve it. Where entertainment media evolved, we have tried to adapt to them.

Some thought we hadn't gone far enough—that parents couldn't spot the advisory easily.

So in 1990, we established a uniform, universally recognizable Parental Advisory logo. It is one inch by a half-inch on cassettes and CD jewel boxes.

There is nothing wrong with [record] companies leaving the decision to parents to determine what their kids should own.

We have launched extensive marketing campaigns to educate both parents and retailers about the system.

With the advent of the Internet, we recently created standards for applying the Parental Advisory logo to on-line sales.

We worked with retailers to use the logo in the way they feel best squares with their own values and needs. Some retailers, for example, chose not to sell recordings carrying the Parental Advisory logo to minors. We cooperate with this decision.

Indeed, we welcome it as an indication that this system is working precisely as we intended it—by giving people the information they need to make their *own* decisions based on their *own* values.

Our most recent attempt to fine-tune this system will take effect just over two weeks from now, on October 1, with the implementation of RIAA's new guidelines for the Parental Advisory label.

The revised guidelines cover the following areas.

First, they provide uniform standards to guide a label and artist in deciding whether to apply the Parental Advisory logo. They advise that this decision be made by weighing contemporary cultural morals. They clarify that the logo should be applied to single-track recordings when they are commercially released as well as full albums.

Second, these guidelines indicate that the Parental Advisory logo should be applied in *all* advertising of a recording that carries the logo.

Finally, we created Internet guidelines for the first time. These guidelines call for a specific display of a parental advisory logo for on-line sales. The Parental Advisory should be visible from the catalog pages all the way through to the shopping basket.

Today, the recording industry's system has taken root in the public mind and the popular culture. They are instantly recognized. And 74% of parents say they are effective.

So what did the FTC find?

From what I can tell, the FTC's findings can be summed up in few sentences. Parents are satisfied with the industry's rating systems to the extent that 74% said so, but the FTC is not. The majority of CD's that carried the sticker were also available in edited form. As far as I can tell, there was one—I repeat one—specific incident of a television program where this music was advertised with a majority under 17 years of age audience and three more that were questionable. Hardly a sweeping industry condemnation. Indeed, since our guidelines are only voluntary and have never contained any age specific restrictions, there is nothing wrong with these companies leaving the decision to parents to determine what their kids should own.

There were a few instances where an album was seemingly marketed to younger teens (the actual specifics are not in the report) although since the FTC report does not delineate whether or not those albums had edited versions available, it is impossible to draw the conclusion that younger teens were subjected to anything that might have been inappropriate.

The report also says that all of its conclusions were reached prior to having the revised guidelines issued by the RIAA, which addresses these concerns.

The principle and most accurate criticism in the FTC report with regard to music is that record retailers each handle the sale of stickered product to young people in different ways. Some don't sell any stickered product at all and others will sell to most anyone. I understand that this is viewed as an "enforcement" problem but in reality, there is nothing that prevents retailers from determining their own policies based on their own local community standards for themselves and their customers. In any event, it is not something over which record companies have or want to have any control.

The American Academy of Child and Adolescent Psychiatry lists 14 signs to look for in a suicidal violent child. Music choices are not among them.

The FTC recommends three things that all of the industry should do:
1. Establish guidelines for advertising—we have.
2. Increase compliance at retail—retailers make their own decisions.
3. Increase parental understanding of the label—77% of the people have said that they are aware but we can always do more education.

Music is just music

Those whose concern for our children is most sincere have the greatest interest in ensuring the problem violence is tackled at its real source. And Mr. Chairman, music recordings are not that source.

I wish it were possible to alter depression or anger through musical lyrics. If it were, you would see a flood of songs urging kids to seek help.

But the American Academy of Child and Adolescent Psychiatry lists 14 signs to look for in a suicidal violent child. Music choices are not among them.

The committee will hear today from experts who posit a correlation between violent behavior and explicit lyrics. That is to say that both occur at the same time—that some youth who listen to music with explicit lyrics also behave violently.

I leave it to people whose expertise in psychology and psychiatry exceeds my own to pontificate on the subject but there simply are no factual correlative studies. We have done the research. In fact, so has the FTC. They said so in this report.

Indeed, the best evidence is experience, and experience in this case is clear. Behind me, Mr. Chairman, are two charts. One shows music sales rising by 4% between 1994 and 1999, and the other shows violent crime among youth falling 27% over the same period. They are not related and that is the point.

The fact is that some people just don't like the music. And that, is a freedom of expression issue.

Another statistic that is not on a chart but is well known to any elected official is that voting among young people is at an all time low. I have spent much of my career encouraging young people to get involved in the political process. To stand up for their future and to talk to politicians about issues they care about. But young people are a smart and cynical bunch today. They don't like it when their culture is attacked even when it is in the guide of corporate responsibility.

A bipartisan survey by Garin-Hart Research and American Viewpoint showed this disconnect among the generations on the issue of culture. When parents were asked what most influenced their kids, they said, television, movies, the Internet, games, music and their friends. When teenagers were asked, they said overwhelmingly, parents, teachers and their church were the most important influences on their lives.

I am sympathetic with parents who feel that their children are no longer under their moral control. But it just isn't the case.

When we take culture that we don't understand and ascribe power and motivation to it that is well beyond how its audience receives it we do a disservice to young people. Young people who continue to need the guidance and leadership of adults in their lives. It is simply wrong to suggest that any government regulatory action can substitute for such involvement, particularly when it comes to art.

An issue for parents, not government

This debate over music keeps coming back to the same thing. Despite all of the trappings and new ways to look at the issue, the fact is that some people just don't like the music. And that, is a freedom of expression issue.

The committee is concerned about violent and sexual lyrics. As a parent, so am I. But I want to apply my *own* values—the needs of my *individual* children—to decide what sources of entertainment are appropriate for them.

If we attempt to apply any other standard, no bonfire will be tall enough to burn the centuries of art that will have to go up in flames.

If violence is inherently demeaning to culture, then Verdi's *Rigolletto*—in which he opens a sack to find it contains his dying daughter—belongs on the pyre. So does Strauss's *Salome*—in which Herod presents Salome with the head of John the Baptist on a platter. For that matter the recent Dixie Chicks song where a wife exacts revenge for an abusive spouse by poisoning his food is in theory equally violent. A new Steve Earle song talks about a death row killer and his crimes and the value of life and death.

Incidentally, nobody has asked for an advisory label on those CD's.

I fully understand those who with utter sincerity feel there is a difference between rap lyrics and grand opera or country music. But there really isn't.

But remember that these artists were criticized in their day. So were others like them, from Picasso to Stravinsky, Flaubert to James Joyce, Charlie Chaplin to Lenny Bruce to George Carlin to Imus—were also dismissed in their time. Classics are rarely recognized in the momentary heat of controversy.

And remember that the distinction between high art and the low road is deeply rooted in individual values and perspectives.

For each person who believes rap lyrics portray a foreign world, there is another who finds them deep and powerful because that world is all too real.

Protecting freedom of expression *and* children

And above all, we must remember this: In our country, expression is not required to pass any test of validity, or even propriety, to be both permitted and protected.

After all, the test of whether America allows free speech is not whether it grants freedom to those with whom we *mildly* disagree. It is whether we protect the freedom of those whose views—and language—make us apoplectic.

Still, I testify today in a spirit of confidence and cooperation—because I speak here as both an executive and a parent.

I care as deeply and passionately about my own children as I know you do about your own. So do my colleagues in the recording industry, from artists to executives.

The real test of commitment to our youth is not how strongly each participant in this discussion can defend its positions or papers, but whether every party can work together to address the complex blend of challenges facing our children.

The last 15 years have proven that we can. And I am confident that we can do so for decades to come. Thank you.

11

Media Violence Makes People More Violent

Gregg Easterbrook

Gregg Easterbrook is a senior editor of the New Republic, *a monthly magazine of politics, foreign policy, and culture.*

Many research studies have found a link between viewing media violence and engaging in real-life violence. For children, there is no question that movie and television violence has a serious effect on children's propensity to behave violently later in life. Until age nineteen, children and teens exposed to media violence are more likely to view violence as a normal behavior and to become criminals themselves.

Millions of teens have seen the 1996 movie *Scream,* a box-office and home-rental hit. Critics adored the film. The *Washington Post* declared that it "deftly mixes irony, self-reference, and social wry commentary." The *Los Angeles Times* hailed it as "a bravura, provocative send-up." *Scream* opens with a scene in which a teenage girl is forced to watch her jock boyfriend tortured and then disemboweled by two fellow students who, it will eventually be learned, want revenge on anyone from high school who crossed them. After jock boy's stomach is shown cut open and he dies screaming, the killers stab and torture the girl, then cut her throat and hang her body from a tree so that Mom can discover it when she drives up. A dozen students and teachers are graphically butchered in the film, while the characters make running jokes about murder. At one point, a boy tells a big-breasted friend she'd better be careful because the stacked girls always get it in horror films; in the next scene, she's grabbed, stabbed through the breasts, and murdered. Some provocative send-up, huh? The movie builds to a finale in which one of the killers announces that he and his accomplice started off by murdering strangers but then realized it was a lot more fun to kill their friends.

Now that two Colorado high schoolers have murdered twelve classmates and a teacher—often, it appears, first taunting their pleading victims, just like celebrity stars do in the movies!—some commentators have dismissed the role of violence in the images shown to the young, pointing out that horrific acts by children existed before celluloid or the phosphor screen. That is true—the Leopold-Loeb murder of 1924, for example. But mass murders by the young, once phenomenally rare, are suddenly on the increase. Can it be coincidence that this increase is happening at the same time that Hollywood has begun to market the notion that mass murder is fun?

Murder as sport

For, in cinema's never-ending quest to up the ante on violence, murder as sport is the latest frontier. Slasher flicks began this trend; most portray carnage from the killer's point of view, showing the victim cowering, begging, screaming as the blade goes in, treating each death as a moment of festivity for the killer. (Many killers seek feelings of power over their victims, criminology finds; by reveling in the pleas of victims, slasher movies promote this base emotion.) The 1994 movie *Natural Born Killers* depicted slaying the helpless not only as a way to have a grand time but also as a way to become a celebrity; several dozen onscreen murders are shown in that film, along with a discussion of how great it makes you feel to just pick people out at random and kill them. The 1994 movie *Pulp Fiction* presented hit men as glamour figures having loads of interesting fun; the actors were mainstream stars like John Travolta. The 1995 movie *Seven,* starring Brad Pitt, portrayed a sort of contest to murder in unusually grotesque ways. (Screenwriters now actually discuss, and critics comment on, which film's killings are most amusing.) The 1995 movie *The Basketball Diaries* contains an extended dream sequence in which the title character, played by teen heartthrob Leonardo DiCaprio, methodically guns down whimpering, pleading classmates at his high school. A rock soundtrack pulses, and the character smiles as he kills.

Mass murders by the young, once phenomenally rare, are suddenly on the increase.

The new Hollywood tack of portraying random murder as a form of recreation does not come from schlock-houses. Disney's Miramax division, the same mainstream studio that produced *Shakespeare in Love,* is responsible for *Scream* and *Pulp Fiction.* Time-Warner is to blame for *Natural Born Killers* and actually ran television ads promoting this film as "delirious, daredevil fun." (After it was criticized for calling murder "fun," Time-Warner tried to justify *Killers* as social commentary; if you believe that, you believe *Godzilla* was really about biodiversity protection.) Praise and publicity for gratuitously violent movies come from the big media conglomerates, including the newspapers and networks that profit from advertising for films that glorify murder. Disney, now one of the leading promoters of violent images in American culture, even feels that what little kids need is more violence. Its Christmas 1998 children's movie *Mighty Joe Young* begins with an eight-year-old girl watching her mother being murdered. By the movie's end, it is 20 years later, and the killer has returned to stalk the grown daughter, pointing a gun in her face and announcing, "Now join your mother in hell." A Disney movie.

One reason Hollywood keeps reaching for ever-more-obscene levels of killing is that it must compete with television, which today routinely airs the kind of violence once considered shocking in theaters. According to studies conducted at Temple University, prime-time network (non-news) shows now average up to five violent acts per hour. In February 1999, NBC ran in prime time the movie *Eraser*, not editing out an extremely graphic scene in which a killer pulls a gun on a bystander and blasts away. The latest TV movie based on *The Rockford Files*, which aired on CBS the night of the Colorado murders, opened with a scene of an eleven-year-old girl in short-shorts being stalked by a man in a black hood, grabbed, and dragged off, screaming. *The Rockford Files* is a comedy. Combining television and movies, the typical American boy or girl, studies find, will observe a stunning 40,000 dramatizations of killing by age 18.

The postwar murder rise in the United States began roughly a decade after TV viewing became common.

In the days after the Colorado slaughter, discussion of violent images in American culture was dominated by the canned positions of the anti-Hollywood right and the mammon-is-our-God film lobby. The debate missed three vital points: the distinction between what adults should be allowed to see (anything) and what the inchoate minds of children and adolescents should see; the way in which important liberal battles to win free expression in art and literature have been perverted into an excuse for antisocial video brutality produced by cynical capitalists; and the difference between censorship and voluntary acts of responsibility.

What the research shows

The day after the Colorado shooting, Mike De Luca, an executive of New Line Cinema, maker of *The Basketball Diaries*, told *USA Today* that, when kids kill, "bad home life, bad parenting, having guns in the home" are "more of a factor than what we put out there for entertainment." Setting aside the disclosure that Hollywood now categorizes scenes of movie stars gunning down the innocent as "entertainment," De Luca is correct: studies do show that upbringing is more determinant of violent behavior than any other factor. But research also clearly shows that the viewing of violence can cause aggression and crime. So the question is, in a society already plagued by poor parenting and unlimited gun sales, why does the entertainment industry feel privileged to make violence even more prevalent?

Even when researchers factor out other influences such as parental attention, many peer-reviewed studies have found causal links between viewing phony violence and engaging in actual violence. A 1971 surgeon general's report asserted a broad relationship between the two. Studies by Brandon Centerwall, an epidemiologist at the University of Wisconsin, have shown that the postwar murder rise in the United States began roughly a decade after TV viewing became common. Centerwall also found that, in South Africa, where television was not generally available until 1975, national murder rates started rising about a decade later. Violent computer games have not existed long enough to be the subject of many controlled studies, but experts expect it will be shown that playing such games in youth also correlates with destructive behavior. There's an eerie likelihood that violent movies and violent games amplify one another, the film and television images placing thoughts of carnage into the psyche while the games condition the trigger finger to act on those impulses.

Kids learn by observation. . . . If what they observe is violent, that's what they learn.

Leonard Eron, a psychologist at the University of Michigan, has been tracking video violence and actual violence for almost four decades. His initial studies, in 1960, found that even the occasional violence depicted in 1950s television—to which every parent would gladly return today—caused increased aggression among eight-year-olds. By the adult years, Eron's studies find, those who watched the most TV and movies in childhood were much more likely to have been arrested for, or convicted of, violent felonies. Eron believes that ten percent of U.S. violent crime is caused by exposure to images of violence, meaning that ninety percent is not but that a ten percent national reduction in violence might be achieved merely by moderating the content of television and movies. "Kids learn by observation," Eron says. "If what they observe is violent, that's what they learn." To cite a minor but telling example, the introduction of vulgar language into American public discourse traces, Eron thinks, largely to the point at which stars like Clark Gable began to swear onscreen, and kids then imitated swearing as normative.

Defenders of bloodshed in film, television, and writing often argue that depictions of killing don't incite real violence because no one is really affected by what they see or read; it's all just water off a duck's back. At heart, this is an argument against free expression. The whole reason to have a First Amendment is that people are influenced by what they see and hear: words and images do change minds, so there must be free competition among them. If what we say, write, or show has no consequences, why bother to have free speech?

Children are more affected by media violence

Defenders of Hollywood bloodshed also employ the argument that, since millions of people watch screen mayhem and shrug, feigned violence has no causal relation to actual violence. After a horrific 1992 case in which a British gang acted out a scene from the slasher movie *Child's Play 3*, torturing a girl to death as the movie had shown, the novelist Martin Amis wrote dismissively in *The New Yorker* that he had rented *Child's Play 3* and watched the film, and it hadn't made him want to kill anyone, so what was the problem? But Amis isn't homicidal or unbalanced. For those on the psychological borderline, the calculus is different. There have, for example, been at least two instances of real-world shootings in which the guilty imitated scenes in *Natural Born Killers.*

Most telling, Amis wasn't affected by watching a slasher movie because Amis is not young. Except for the unbalanced, exposure to violence in video "is not so important for adults; adults can watch anything they want," Eron says. Younger minds are a different story. Children who don't yet understand the difference between illusion and reality may be highly affected by video violence. Between the ages of two and eight, hours of viewing violent TV programs and movies correlates closely to felonies later in life; the child comes to see hitting, stabbing, and shooting as normative acts. The link between watching violence and engaging in violence continues up to about the age of 19, Eron finds, after which most people's characters have been formed, and video mayhem no longer correlates to destructive behavior.

Blaming guns—while also glamorizing them

Trends in gun availability do not appear to explain the murder rise that has coincided with television and violent films. Research by John Lott Jr., of the University of Chicago Law School, shows that the percentage of homes with guns has changed little throughout the postwar era. What appears to have changed is the willingness of people to fire their guns at one another. Are adolescents now willing to use guns because violent images make killing seem acceptable or even cool? Following the Colorado slaughter, the *New York Times* ran a recounting of other postwar mass murders staged by the young, such as the 1966 Texas tower killings, and noted that they all happened before the advent of the Internet or shock rock, which seemed to the *Times* to absolve the modern media. But all the mass killings by the young occurred after 1950—after it became common to watch violence on television.

Children who don't yet understand the difference between illusion and reality may be highly affected by video violence.

When horrific murders occur, the film and television industries routinely attempt to transfer criticism to the weapons used. Just after the Colorado shootings, for instance, TV talk-show host Rosie O'Donnell called for a constitutional amendment banning all firearms. How strange that O'Donnell didn't call instead for a boycott of Sony or its production company, Columbia Tristar—a film studio from which she has received generous paychecks and whose current offerings include *8MM*, which glamorizes the sexual murder of young women, and *The Replacement Killers,* whose hero is a hit man and which depicts dozens of gun murders. Handguns should be licensed, but that hardly excuses the convenient sanctimony of blaming the crime on the weapon, rather than on what resides in the human mind.

And, when it comes to promoting adoration of guns, Hollywood might as well be the NRA's marketing arm. An everincreasing share of film and television depicts the firearm as something the virile must have and use, if not an outright sexual aid. Check the theater section of any newspaper, and you will find an ever-higher percentage of movie ads in which the stars are prominently holding guns. Keanu Reeves, Uma Thurman, Laurence Fishburne, Geena Davis, Woody Harrelson, and Mark Wahlberg are just a few of the hip stars who have posed with guns for movie advertising. Hollywood endlessly congratulates itself for reducing the depiction of cigarettes in movies and movie ads. Cigarettes had to go, the film industry admitted, because glamorizing them gives the wrong idea to kids. But the glamorization of firearms, which is far more dangerous, continues. Today, even female stars who otherwise consider themselves politically aware will model in sexualized poses with guns. Ads for the . . . movie *Goodbye Lover* show star Patricia Arquette nearly nude, with very little between her and the viewer but her handgun.

The profitability of violent cinema

But doesn't video violence merely depict a stark reality against which the young need be warned? American society is far too violent, yet the forms of brutality highlighted in the movies and on television—prominently "thrill" killings and serial murders—are pure distortion. Nearly 99 percent of real murders result from robberies, drug deals, and domestic disputes; figures from research affiliated with the FBI's behavioral sciences division show an average of only about 30 serial or "thrill" murders nationally per year. Thirty is plenty horrifying enough, but, at this point, each of the major networks and movie studios alone depicts more "thrill" and serial murders annually than that. By endlessly exploiting the notion of the "thrill" murder, Hollywood and television present to the young an entirely imaginary image of a society in which killing for pleasure is a common event. The publishing industry, including some TNR advertisers, also distorts for profit the frequency of "thrill" murders.

When it comes to promoting adoration of guns, Hollywood might as well be the [National Rifle Association's] marketing arm.

The profitability of violent cinema is broadly dependent on the "down-rating" of films—movies containing extreme violence being rated only R instead of NC-17 (the new name for X)—and the lax enforcement of age restrictions regarding movies. Teens are the best market segment for Hollywood; when moviemakers claim their violent movies are not meant to appeal to teens, they are simply lying. The millionaire status of actors, directors, and studio heads—and the returns of the mutual funds that invest in movie companies—depends on not restricting teen access to theaters or film rentals. Studios in effect control the movie ratings board and endlessly lobby it not to label extreme violence with an NC-17, the only form of rating that is actually enforced. *Natural Born Killers*, for example, received an R following Time-Warner lobbying, despite its repeated close-up murders and one charming scene in which the stars kidnap a high school girl and argue about whether it would be more fun to kill her before or after raping her. Since its inception, the movie ratings board has put its most restrictive rating on any realistic representation of lovemaking, while sanctioning ever-more-graphic depictions of murder and torture. In economic terms, the board's pro-violence bias gives studios an incentive to present more death and mayhem, confident that ratings officials will smile with approval.

When R-and-X battles were first fought, intellectual sentiment regarded the ratings system as a way of blocking the young from seeing films with political content, such as *Easy Rider,* or discouraging depictions of sexuality; ratings were perceived as the rubes' counterattack against cinematic sophistication. But, in the 1960s, murder after murder after murder was not standard cinema fare. The most controversial violent film of that era, *A Clockwork Orange,* depicted a total of one killing, which was heard but not on-camera. (*Clockwork Orange* also had genuine political content, unlike most of today's big-studio movies.) In an era of runaway screen violence, the '60s ideal that the young should be allowed to see what they want has been corrupted. In this, trends in video mirror the misuse of liberal ideals generally.

Hollywood and television present to the young an entirely imaginary image of a society in which killing for pleasure is a common event.

Anti-censorship battles of the twentieth century were fought on firm ground, advocating the right of films to tackle social and sexual issues (the 1930s Hays office forbid among other things cinematic mention of cohabitation) and free access to works of literature such as *Ulysses, Story of O,* and the original version of Norman Mailer's *The Naked and the Dead.* Struggles against censors established that suppression of film or writing is wrong.

But to say that nothing should be censored is very different from saying that everything should be shown. Today, Hollywood and television have twisted the First Amendment concept that occasional repulsive or worthless expression must be protected, so as to guarantee freedom for works of genuine political content or artistic merit, into a new standard in which constitutional freedoms are employed mainly to safeguard works that make no pretense of merit. In the new standard, the bulk of what's being protected is repulsive or worthless, with the meritorious work the rare exception.

Not only is there profit for the performers, producers, management, and shareholders of firms that glorify violence, so, too, is there profit for politicians. Many conservative or Republican politicians who denounce Hollywood eagerly accept its lucre. Bob Dole's 1995 anti-Hollywood speech was not followed up by any anti-Hollywood legislation or campaign-funds strategy. After the Colorado murders, President Clinton declared, "Parents should take this moment to ask what else they can do to shield children from violent images and experiences that warp young perceptions." But Clinton was careful to avoid criticizing Hollywood, one of the top sources of public backing and campaign contributions for him and his would-be successor, Vice President Al Gore. The president had nothing specific to propose on film violence—only that parents should try to figure out what to do.

A call for restraint

When television producers say it is the parents' obligation to keep children away from the tube, they reach the self-satire point of warning that their own product is unsuitable for consumption. The situation will improve somewhat beginning in 2000, by which time all new TVs must be sold with the "V chip"—supported by Clinton and Gore—which will allow parents to block violent shows. But it will be at least a decade before the majority of the nation's sets include the chip, and who knows how adept young minds will prove at defeating it? Rather than relying on a technical fix that will take many years to achieve an effect, TV producers could simply stop churning out the gratuitous violence. Television could dramatically reduce its output of scenes of killing and still depict violence in news broadcasts, documentaries, and the occaional show in which the horrible is genuinely relevant. Reduction in violence is not censorship; it is placing social responsibility before profit.

The movie industry could practice the same kind of restraint without sacrificing profitability. In this regard, the big Hollywood studios, including Disney, look craven and exploitative compared to, of all things, the porn-video industry. Repulsive material occurs in underground porn, but, in the products sold by the mainstream triple-X distributors such as Vivid Video (the MGM of the erotica business), violence is never, ever, ever depicted—because that would be irresponsible. Women and men perform every conceivable explicit act in today's mainstream porn, but what is shown is always consensual and almost sunnily friendly. Scenes of rape or sexual menace never occur, and scenes of sexual murder are an absolute taboo.

It is beyond irony that today Sony and Time-Warner eagerly market explicit depictions of women being raped, sexually assaulted, and sexually murdered, while the mainstream porn industry would never dream of doing so. But, if money is all that matters, the point here is that mainstream porn is violence-free and yet risqué and highly profitable. Surely this shows that Hollywood could voluntarily step back from the abyss of glorifying violence and still retain its edge and its income.

Following the Colorado massacre, 2000 Republican presidential candidate Gary Bauer declared to a campaign audience, "In the America I want, all of these producers and directors, they would not be able to show their faces in public" because fingers "would be pointing at them and saying, 'Shame, shame.'" The statement sent chills through anyone fearing right-wing thought-control. But Bauer's final clause is correct—Hollywood and television do need to hear the words "shame, shame." The cause of the shame should be removed voluntarily, not to stave off censorship, but because it is the responsible thing to do.

Put it this way. The day after a teenager guns down the sons and daughters of studio executives in a high school in Bel Air or Westwood, Disney and Time-Warner will stop glamorizing murder. Do we have to wait until that day?

12

The Entertainment Industry Markets Violent Media to Children

Charlie Condon

Charlie Condon is the attorney general of South Carolina.

A 2000 report from the Federal Trade Commission confirmed what parents have long suspected: that the advertising for violent movies, television shows, video games, and music CDs intentionally targets young audiences. When it comes to marketing their products, the movie, TV, video game, and music industries ignore their own rating systems that are designed to warn parents about which products are inappropriate for children. Entertainment industry executives say that their violent material is for adult audiences, but in reality they market this harmful material to children.

In September 2000, America heard the proverbial fire bell in the night. The Federal Trade Commission's (FTC's) stunning report, *Marketing Violent Entertainment to Children,* sounded the alarm by exposing with impressive particularity the devastating impact that Hollywood entertainment is having upon America's children.

This report is an indictment of Hollywood's pernicious practice of targeting children to attract them to violent, sex-filled movies, games and music. While it always was suspected that Hollywood had zeroed in on the teen-age audience to fill its coffers, the FTC now delivers to us the smoking gun. Hollywood moguls have left no stone unturned, even targeting the Camp Fire Girls.

Hollywood vs. the American family

The specifics of the report are frightening, especially to parents. The agency's findings explain in part why America's family unit is being overwhelmed and undermined. While it certainly is true that parents must play the central role in teaching the child right from wrong, there also is little doubt that Hollywood relentlessly is pursuing the teen-age audience with the lure of the lurid. Like acid, Hollywood's repeated exposure of children to violence and sex eats away at the family structure.

Consider these findings. Eighty percent of the R-rated films examined targeted youth younger than 17 years old. Nine of the 20 PG-13 films studied by the FTC went after children 11 and younger. Free passes for movie screenings and free merchandise, such as T-shirts and posters, were given away where teens regularly hung out. Of 118 video games with a "mature" rating for violence, 70 percent were advertised and promoted to children younger than 17. Based on FTC analysis, almost one-half of those too young for R-rated movies got tickets to see these films.

The [Federal Trade Commission] has caught Hollywood red-handed attracting our children to violent and sexually explicit forms of so-called "entertainment."

Backed by this data, no wonder the FTC concluded that "members of the motion-picture, music-recording and electronic-game industries routinely target children under 17 as the audience for movies, music and games that they themselves acknowledge are inappropriate for children." In other words, Hollywood is sanctimoniously saying that certain entertainment is inappropriate for youngsters, while at the same time aggressively enticing those youngsters to the very movies, music or games the industry has publicly declared off-limits. Chasing the almighty dollar, Hollywood is using sex, violence and our children as its vehicle for pursuit.

The solutions suggested in response to the FTC's highly disturbing findings all have been heard before. The FTC itself has called upon Hollywood to voluntarily stop targeting impressionable teen-agers with violence-laced products. Many say we must work with industry leaders to obtain a "cease-fire" on our children. Others urge more and better industry self-regulation, particularly since Hollywood's detrimental practice of targeting youth is covered by the First Amendment. In addition, most emphasize that parents, not government, must shoulder primary responsibility for protecting their children from entertainment obviously inappropriate for younger audiences.

I would hope these solutions produce immediate, positive results. But for a problem so pervasive as Hollywood's assault upon America's families, I am afraid we no longer can rely upon hopes unfulfilled and promises unkept. Thus far, self-regulation by the entertainment industry has been an utter failure. Moreover, to those of us responsible for enforcing existing laws, saying we must await the entertainment industry's regulation of itself is like saying that because there are more basic solutions for stopping drug dealing—such as prevention and education—a police officer should just ignore drug dealers caught in the act. That is ludicrous.

The FTC has caught Hollywood red-handed attracting our children to violent and sexually explicit forms of so-called "entertainment." Current laws protect us against these abominable practices. Those laws must be enforced.

Harming youth

Like the Pied Piper, Hollywood is leading our children toward destruction. The FTC recognized that "a majority of the investigations into the impact of media violence on children find that there is a high correlation between exposure to media violence and aggressive and, at times, violent behavior." Violent entertainment unquestionably is linked to violence in real life.

There have been too many tragedies lately which bear this out only too well. While countless other factors are at work when teen-agers resort to violent outbursts, can we seriously suggest that the video game Doom played no role in the Columbine High School massacre in Littleton, Colorado? Of course not.

Can anyone earnestly argue that *The Basketball Diaries* movie played no significance in the gunning down of eight innocent victims in Paducah, Kentucky? Obviously, no. The Paducah shooter was highly skilled in video-game play. Incredibly, he was eight for eight in hitting his victims.

Certain teen-agers are high risks for violent behavior. They can be pushed over the edge by Hollywood-produced trash that touches the child's hot buttons through glorified violence. To argue Hollywood has no culpability for this kind of violent entertainment is to live in the same kind of dream world created for teen-agers by many of today's violent movies, video games and gangster-rap music. Wholesale violence is addictive and, if left unchecked, it completely will overwhelm the moral teachings of parents.

Movie director Sydney Pollack recently was quoted as saying that "as long as there's an appetite, the industry will feed it." Rapper Eminem spews the venomous words "I'ma Kill You" as if they were a light-hearted lyric. He degrades women and glorifies mass murder. Jack Valenti, president of the Motion Picture Association of America, has boasted, "There is no enterprise in America that is more attentive to the parents of this country than the movie industry." This is not true. None of these references lend much comfort to the belief that Hollywood will change its ways anytime soon.

Hollywood acknowledges that certain material is inappropriate for youngsters, yet aggressively lures them to the very harmful materials that it has warned against.

Everyone agrees that parents must assume primary responsibility for their children's behavior. But parents must not be undermined in their parental roles, either. When Hollywood, using its financial wealth and slick ads to excite, hypnotize and entice youngsters, subverts parental authority through deceptive and unfair practices, then we have the responsibility to enforce existing laws banning such practices.

Clearly, what we have here is a virtual replay—only much worse—of the damage the tobacco industry did to our children. But instead of Joe Camel, Hollywood is using Eminem, *South Park,* Doom and people such as film director Quentin Tarantino to seduce children and subvert parents.

What makes Hollywood's actions more intolerable and its conduct more sinister even than that of the tobacco industry is that Hollywood acknowledges that certain entertainment is inappropriate for youngsters, yet aggressively lures them to the very harmful materials it has warned against. Such conduct is hypocritical, deceptive and detrimental to our children. Unless we act, Hollywood's power and influence will just keep on increasing.

Hollywood has set a trap for our youth and springs it every day with a new movie, a new game or a new CD, each more lurid, shocking, senseless and violent than the last.

What we can do while awaiting responsible self-regulation from Hollywood executives or new action by Congress is enforce the laws already on the books against Hollywood. South Carolina, like most states, forbids deceptive and unfair business practices. Hollywood corporate executives say one thing, but do another. They outwardly restrict entertainment, yet in reality promote damaging material to teen-agers. Their conduct has all the makings of an unfair trade practice. When Hollywood disseminates and distributes entertainment that violates our statutes protecting minors from harmful and indecent materials, we must enforce those laws.

Using the courts

That is why I have asked fellow state attorneys general to consider joint legal action against Hollywood. Together, through lawsuits, state attorneys general changed the practices of the tobacco industry forever. In addition to compensation for the wrongs committed, the tobacco industry was required to take specific, affirmative steps to stop targeting teen-agers with tobacco products.

Likewise, we state attorneys general must hit Hollywood where it hurts—in the courts and in the pocketbook. Like tobacco, we can require this irresponsible industry to act responsibly. For example, Hollywood must stop its marketing to children of T-shirts and other paraphernalia for the promotion of movies inappropriate for them to see. It must stop using 10-year-olds as its research tool for marketing new R-rated movies. It must find a way to prevent R-rated movie trailers from being shown to children. Hollywood must start taking affirmative steps in the community to ensure children do not gain access to R-rated or "mature" materials. The entertainment industry must accept the responsibility of being a good corporate citizen just like every other business. For a change, the entertainment industry must take parents' views into account. In short, the Hollywood entertainment industry must recognize the simple truth that just because it can make a buck off a child doesn't mean it should.

I oppose using lawsuits or the courthouse to replace the legislative process in Congress or the statehouse. But here, we have laws already on the books forbidding unfair trade practices and dissemination of materials harmful to minors. Hollywood, like any other business, needs to know we also mean business.

We cannot afford another Littleton or Paducah. One more round fired in the hallways or the classrooms is one too many. Nor can we afford for the moral fiber of our children to be destroyed by shock entertainment which assaults the conscience. Hollywood, however, can afford to pay for the wrongs it has committed. While the Hollywood entertainment industry believes nothing can or will be done to rein it in, grassroots America is rising in anger and demanding action.

Hollywood has set a trap for our youth and springs it every day with a new movie, a new game or a new CD, each more lurid, shocking, senseless and violent than the last. Nothing will be done, no change in irresponsible behavior will occur, until we see Hollywood executives inside a courtroom. Hollywood's practice of targeting youth is hitting the American family between the eyes. It must be stopped.

13

The Problem of Media Violence Is Not Serious Enough to Justify Censorship

Wendy Kaminer

Wendy Kaminer frequently writes for the American Prospect *and other publications on civil liberties, feminism, and religion in America. She is the author of several books, including* Sleeping with Extra-Terrestrials: The Rise of Irrationalism and Perils of Piety.

In the 2000 presidential race, democratic candidate Al Gore, his running mate Joseph Lieberman, and several other politicians called for legislation to regulate the advertising of violent entertainment. No such legislation passed, which is fortunate because it would have dealt a serious blow to free speech. There is no solid evidence that violent entertainment causes violence, so government censorship of material is not justified. Censoring violent entertainment simply because it is unpopular would set a dangerous precedent that would threaten speech about other politically sensitive issues, such as abortion or homosexuality.

Like Claude Rains in *Casablanca,* [2000 presidential candidate] Al Gore is shocked!, shocked! that the entertainment industry is marketing violent material to minors. Countering Hollywood's macho entertainments with some macho rhetoric of his own, he gave the industry six months to "clean up its act" and declare a "ceasefire" in what he apparently sees as the media's war against America's children.

No one should be surprised by the vice president's threat to impose government regulations on the marketing of popular entertainments, which immediately followed the issuance of a new Federal Trade Commission (FTC) report on the subject. As his choice of running mate [Joseph Lieberman] made clear, Gore is positioning himself as the moral voice of the Democratic Party—replete with Godliness and a desire to cleanse the culture. With a concomitant promise to protect ordinary Americans from rapacious corporations, Gore is an early twenty-first-century version of a nineteenth-century female Progressive—a God-loving social purist with a soft spot for working families and, not so incidentally, women's rights.

The push to censor "toxic" media

Many Victorian women's rights activists, like Frances Willard of the Women's Christian Temperance Union and Julia Ward Howe, enthusiastically supported the suppression of "impure" or "vicious" literature, which was blamed for corrupting the nation's youth. "Books are feeders for brothels" according to the notorious nineteenth-century antivice crusader Anthony Comstock, for whom the nation's first obscenity law was named. Gun violence is fed by violent media, Al Gore, Joseph Lieberman, and others assert. The new FTC report was commissioned by President Clinton immediately after the 1999 shootings at Columbine High. That was when centrist politicians (and commentators) were touting the new "commonsense" view of youth violence: It was caused by both the availability of firearms and the availability of violent media. Gun control would be complemented by culture control.

So in June 1999, two Democratic senators, Lieberman and the usually thoughtful Kent Conrad of North Dakota, joined with [Senators] Trent Lott and John McCain in proposing federal legislation requiring the labeling of violent audio and visual media. These requirements, which were to be enforced by the FTC, were amendments to the cigarette labeling act. (When politicians revisit their bad ideas, critics like me repeat themselves. I discussed this proposed bill and the bipartisan drive to censor in a November 23, 1999, *American Prospect* column, "The Politics of Sanctimony.")

Advocates of censorship often charge that media can be "toxic". . . . By describing whatever film or CD they disdain as a defective product, they undermine the view of it as speech.

Advocates of censorship often charge that media can be "toxic" (as well as "addictive") like tobacco and other drugs. By describing whatever film or CD they disdain as a defective product, they undermine the view of it as speech. (We should regulate pornography the way we regulate exploding Ford Pintos, one feminist antiporn activist used to say; she seemed to consider *Playboy* an incendiary device.) In endorsing Internet filtering programs, Gore has remarked that minors should be protected from "dangerous places" on the Internet—in other words, "dangerous" speech. Some Web sites should effectively be locked up, just as medicine cabinets are locked up to protect children from poisons, the vice president remarked at a 1997 Internet summit.

Once you define violent or sexually explicit media as toxic products, it is not terribly difficult to justify regulating their advertising, at least, if not their distribution and production. Commercial speech generally enjoys constitutional protection, but as advocates of marketing restrictions assert, the First Amendment does not protect false or misleading advertising or ads promoting illegal activities. That's true but not necessarily relevant here. Campaigns marketing violent entertainment to children may be sleazy, but they don't promote an illegal activity (the sale of violent material to minors is not generally criminal); and they're not deceptive or unfair (many popular entertainments are just as bad as they purport to be). Ratings are not determined or mandated by the government (not yet, anyway), so why should it be a federal offense for industry executives to violate the spirit of their own voluntary codes?

The [Federal Trade Commission] study on which would-be censors rely found no clear causal connection between violent media and violent behavior.

Effective regulation of media marketing campaigns would require new federal legislation that would entangle the government in the production of popular entertainments. What might this legislation entail? Ratings and labeling would be mandatory, supervised by the FTC (or some other federal agency), and any effort to subvert the ratings system would be a federal offense. Testifying before the Senate Commerce Committee on September 12, 2000, Lieberman promised that regulation of the entertainment industry would focus on "how they market, not what they produce," but that promise ignores the effect of marketing considerations on content.

The dangers of censorship

Some may consider the decline of violent entertainments no great loss, imagining perhaps that slasher movies and violent video games will be the primary victims of a new federal labeling regime. But it's not hard to imagine a docudrama about domestic abuse or abortion, or a coming-of-age story about a gay teen, receiving the same restricted rating as a sleazy movie about a serial murderer. In any case, a stringent, federally mandated and monitored rating and labeling system will not enhance parental control; it's a vehicle for bureaucratic control. Federal officials, not parents, will determine what entertainment will be available to children when they devise and enforce the ratings.

Some claim that federal action is justified, nonetheless, by an overriding need to save lives. At the September 12 hearing inspired by the FTC report, several senators and other witnesses vigorously condemned the entertainment industry for "literally making a killing off of marketing to kids," in the words of Kansas Republican Sam Brownback. He called upon the industry to stop producing the entertainments he abhors. Lieberman charged that media violence was "part of a toxic mix that has turned some of our children into killers." Lynne Cheney, former head of the National Endowment for the Humanities, declared that "there is a problem with the product they market, no matter how they market it." Democratic Senator Fritz Hollings proposed giving the Federal Communications Commission the power to impose a partial ban on whatever programming it considers violent and harmful to minors.

What all this hyperbolic rhetoric obscured (or ignored) was the dearth of hard evidence that violent media actually turns "children into killers." In fact, the FTC study on which would-be censors rely found no clear causal connection between violent media and violent behavior. "Exposure to violent materials probably is not even the most important factor" in determining whether a child will turn violent, FTC Chairman Robert Pitofsky observed. The most he would say was that exposure to violent media "does seem to correlate with aggressive attitudes, insensitivity toward violence, and an exaggerated view of how much violence occurs in the world."

This is not exactly a defense of media violence, but it may present a fairly balanced view of its effects, which do not justify limitations on speech. Living in a free society entails a commitment not to prohibit speech unless it clearly, directly, and intentionally causes violence. If violent entertainment can be regulated by the federal government because it allegedly causes violence, so can inflammatory political rhetoric, like assertions that abortion providers kill babies. Anti-abortion rhetoric probably has even a clearer connection to violence than any violent movie, but both must be protected. If Disney can be brought under the thumb of federal regulators, so can Cardinal Law when he denounces abortion as murder.

Living in a free society entails a commitment not to prohibit speech unless it clearly, directly, and intentionally causes violence.

It's unfortunate and ironic that apparently amoral corporations, like Disney or Time-Warner, stand as champions and beneficiaries of First Amendment rights. As gatekeepers of the culture, they're not exactly committed to maintaining an open, diverse marketplace of ideas. Indeed, the de facto censorship engineered by media conglomerates may threaten public discourse nearly as much as federal regulation. And neither our discourse nor our culture is exactly enriched by gratuitously violent media.

But speech doesn't have to provide cultural enrichment to enjoy constitutional protection. We don't need a First Amendment to protect popular, inoffensive speech or speech that a majority of people believe has social value. We need it to protect speech that Lynne Cheney or Joseph Lieberman consider demeaning and degrading. Censorship campaigns often begin with a drive to protect children (or women), but they rarely end there.

Organizations to Contact

The editors have compiled the following list of organizations concerned with the issues debated in this book. The descriptions are derived from materials provided by the organizations. All have publications or information available for interested readers. The list was compiled on the date of publication of the present volume; the information provided here may change. Be aware that many organizations take several weeks or longer to respond to inquiries, so allow as much time as possible.

American Academy of Child and Adolescent Psychiatry (AACAP)
3615 Wisconsin Ave. NW, Washington, DC 20016-3007
(202) 966-7300 • fax: (202) 966-2891
website: www.aacap.org

AACAP is the leading national professional medical organization committed to treating the seven to twelve million American youth suffering from mental, behavioral, and developmental disorders. It publishes the monthly *Journal of the American Academy of Child and Adolescent Psychiatry* and the reports "Children and TV Violence" and "Understanding Violent Behavior in Children and Adolescents."

American Civil Liberties Union (ACLU)
125 Broad St., 18th Fl., New York, NY 10004-2400
(212) 549-2500
website: www.aclu.org

The ACLU is a national organization that works to defend Americans' civil rights as guaranteed by the U.S. Constitution. It opposes the V-chip and the censoring of any form of speech, including media depictions of violence. The ACLU publishes the quarterly newsletter *Civil Liberties Alert* and several handbooks, project reports, civil liberties books, pamphlets, and public policy reports, including "From Words to Weapons: The Violence Surrounding Our Schools" and "The ACLU on Violence Chip."

American Family Association (AFA)
PO Drawer 2440, Tupelo, MS 38803
(601) 844-5036 • fax: (601) 842-7798
website: www.afa.net

The AFA opposes the proliferation of violence, profanity, vulgarity, and pornography in popular entertainment. It sponsors letter-writing campaigns to encourage television sponsors to support only quality programming, and it compiles statistics on how media violence affects society. The association's publications include books, videos, the monthly *AFA Journal*, and the *AFA Action Alert* newsletter.

Center for Media Literacy
4727 Wilshire Blvd., Suite 403, Los Angeles, CA 90010
(800) 226-9494
website: www.medialit.org

The center is a national advocacy organization that distributes educational materials and develops training programs for promoting critical thinking about the media in school classrooms, after-school programs, parent education, religious and community centers, and in the home. It publishes numerous materials about media literacy, including the video *Beyond Blame: Challenging Violence in the Media* and *Who's Calling the Shots: How to Respond Effectively to Children's Fascination with War Play and War Toys.*

Federal Trade Commission (FTC)
CRC-240, Washington, DC 20580
(202) 326-2222
website: www.ftc.gov

The FTC is the government agency charged with promoting free-market competition and monitoring unfair trade practices. On September 11, 2000, in response to the 1999 school shooting in Littleton, Colorado, the FTC released its report *Marketing Violent Entertainment to Children: A Review of Self-Regulation and Industry Practices in the Motion Picture, Music Recording & Electronic Game Industries.*

Media Awareness Network
1500 Merivale Rd., 3rd Fl., Nepean, ON K2E 6Z5 Canada
(800) 896-3342
website: www.media-awareness.ca

The mission of the Media Awareness Network is to promote and support media education in Canadian schools, homes, and communities. Through its Internet site, the network provides both curriculum-related media and web literacy teaching materials. News updates, online articles, and a summary of the Canadian government's response to the problem of media violence are available on the network's website.

Media Coalition
139 Fulton St., Suite 302, New York, NY 10038
(212) 587-4025 • fax: (212) 587-2436
website: www.mediacoalition.org

The Media Coalition defends the First Amendment right to produce and sell books, magazines, recordings, videotapes, and video games. It defends the American public's right to have access to the broadest possible range of opinion and entertainment, including works considered offensive or harmful due to their violent or sexually explicit nature. It opposes the government-mandated ratings system for television. Media Coalition distributes to its members regular reports outlining the activities of Congress, state legislatures, and the courts on issues related to the First Amendment.

Mediascope
12711 Ventura Blvd., Suite 440, Studio City, CA 91604
(818) 508-2080 • fax: (818) 508-2088
website: www.mediascope.org

Mediascope is a nonprofit, public policy organization founded to promote constructive depictions of health and social issues in media. It provides tools and information to help the entertainment community be more socially responsible without relinquishing creative freedom. Mediascope publishes various issue briefs and articles, as well as the reports *Video Games and Their Effects* and *More Than a Movie: Ethics in Entertainment.*

National Coalition Against Censorship (NCAC)
275 Seventh Ave., New York, NY 10001
(212) 807-6222
website: www.ncac.org

NCAC is an alliance of nonprofit organizations working to educate the public about the dangers of censorship and how to oppose it. The collation strives to create a climate of opinion hospitable to First Amendment freedoms. Its website contains articles, testimony, and news updates regarding censorship of violence in the media.

National Coalition on Television Violence (NCTV)
5132 Newport Ave., Bethesda, MD 20816
website: www.nctvv.org

NCTV is a research and education association dedicated to reducing the violence in films and television programming. It distributes ratings, reviews, and violence research. It publishes the quarterly *NCTV News* as well as various reports and educational materials.

Parents Television Council (PTC)
PO Box 712067, Los Angeles, CA 90071-9934
(213) 621-2506
website: www.ParentsTV.org

PTC was established as a special project of the Media Research Center. Its goal is to bring America's demand for values-driven television programming to the entertainment industry. PTC produces an annual *Family Guide to Prime Time Television*, based on scientific monitoring and analysis generated from the Media Research Center's computerized Media Tracking System. The *Family Guide* profiles every sitcom and drama on the major television networks and provides information on subject matter that is inappropriate for children. PTC also publishes various reports, including *A Vanishing Haven: The Decline of the Family Hour.*

TV-Turnoff Network
1611 Connecticut Ave. NW, Suite 3A, Washington, DC 20009
(202) 887-0436 • fax: (202) 518-5560
e-mail: tvfa@essential.org • website: http://www.tvfa.org

The TV-Turnoff Network is a national nonprofit organization that encourages Americans to reduce the amount of television they watch in order to promote stronger families and communities. It sponsors the National TV-Turnoff Week, when more than five million people across the country go without television for seven days.

Bibliography

Books

Sissela Bok

Mayhem: Violence as Public Entertainment. Reading, MA: Addison-Wesley, 1998.

Joanne Cantor

Mommy, I'm Scared: How TV and Movies Frighten Children and What We Can Do to Protect Them. New York: Harcourt Brace, 1998.

Carol J. Clover

Men, Women, and Chain Saws: Gender in the Modern Horror Film. Princeton, NJ: Princeton University Press, 1992.

Denis Duclos

The Werewolf Complex: America's Fascination with Violence. New York: Berg, 1998.

William Dudley, ed.

Media Violence: Opposing Viewpoints. San Diego: Greenhaven Press, 1999.

Jib Fowles

The Case for Television Violence. Thousand Oaks, CA: Sage, 1999.

Cynthia A. Freeland

The Naked and the Undead: Evil and the Appeal of Horror. Boulder, CO: Westview Press, 2000.

James Garbarino

Lost Boys: Why Our Sons Turn Violent and How We Can Save Them. New York: Free Press, 1999.

James William Gibson

Warrior Dreams: Violence and Manhood in Post-Vietnam America. New York: Hill and Wang, 1994.

Jeffrey Goldstein, ed.

Why We Watch: The Attractions of Violent Entertainment. New York: Oxford University Press, 1998.

Dave Grossman and Gloria Degaetano

Stop Teaching Our Kids to Kill: A Call to Action Against TV, Movie, and Video Game Violence. New York: Random House, 1999.

Jake Horsley

The Blood Poets: A Cinema of Savagery 1958–1999. Lanham, MD: Scarecrow Press, 1999.

Carla Brooks Johnston

Screened Out: How the Media Control Us and What We Can Do About It. Armonk, NY: M.E. Sharpe, 2000.

S. Robert Lichter, Linda S. Lichter, and Stanley Rothman

Prime Time: How TV Portrays American Culture. Washington, DC: Regnery, 1994.

Michael Medved

Hollywood vs. America: Popular Culture and the War on Traditional Values. New York: HarperCollins, 1992.

National Television Violence Study. Thousand Oaks, CA: Sage, 1997.

Tom O'Brien   *The Screening of America: Movie Values from* Rocky *to* Rain
                      Man. New York: Continuum, 1990.

Stephen Prince, ed.   *Screening Violence*. New Brunswick: Rutgers University
                      Press, 2000.

James D. Torr, ed.   *Current Controversies: Violence in the Media*. San Diego:
                      Greenhaven Press, 2001.

James B. Twitchell   *Preposterous Violence: Fables of Aggression in Modern Cul-
                      ture*. New York: Oxford University Press, 1989.

Periodicals

Kris Axtman   "Media Violence May Be Easier Tarred Than Regulated,"
                      Christian Science Monitor, September 14, 2000.

Brian Doherty   "Bum Rap," *Reason*, December 2000.

Susan J. Douglas   "The Devil Made Me Do It: Is *Natural Born Killers* the
                      Ford Pinto of Movies?" *The Nation*, April 5, 1999.

Anne P. Dupre   "Violence, Depravity, and the Movies: The Lure of De-
                      viancy," *USA Today*, January 1999.

Charles Gordon   "Much Ado About Media Violence," *Macleans's*, May 24,
                      1999.

Dave Grossman   "Trained to Kill," *Christianity Today*, August 10, 1998.

Gayle M.B. Hanson   "The Violent World of Video Games," *Insight on the
                      News*, June 28, 1999. Available from 3600 New York Ave.
                      NE, Washington, DC 20002.

Thomas L. Jipping   "Diagnosing the Cultural Virus," *World & I*, July 1999.

Paul Keegan   "Culture Quake," *Mother Jones*, November/December
                      1999.

John Leo   "Gunning for Hollywood," *U.S. News & World Report*,
                      May 10, 1999.

Rob Long   "Hollywood, Littleton, and Us," *National Review*, July 26,
                      1999.

Michael Massing   "Movie Violence, Still Playing," *Washington Post*, July 4,
                      1999.

Michael Medved   "Hollywood's 'Popular Culture' Out of Touch," *USA To-
                      day*, October 5, 2000.

Kevin Merida and   "When Death Imitates Art," *Washington Post*, April 22,
Richard Leiby   1999.

Virginia Postrel   "The Creative Matrix: What We Lose by Regulating Cul-
                      ture," *Reason*, August/September 1999.

Richard Rhodes   "Hollow Claims About Fantasy Violence," *New York
                      Times*, September 7, 2000.

John Roman   "It's a Job for Parents, Not the Government," *Newsweek*,
                      August 9, 1999.

Cheri W. Sparks and Glenn G. Sparks   "Why Do Hollywood and TV Keep Showing Us Violence?" *USA Today*, January 2001.

Scott Stossel   "The Man Who Counts the Killings," *Atlantic Monthly*, May 1997.

Ray Surette   "That's Entertainment?" *World & I*, September 1998.

Ray Surette   "The Promise and the Reality—Peddling Violent Entertainment to Children," *World & I*, April 2001.

Index

Acland, Charles, 35, 38
advertisers
   television, effects of controversy on,
      22
Advertising Age (magazine), 27
AFA Journal, 37
age
   as factor in viewing of TV violence,
      35–36
   see also demographics
aggressive behavior. *See* behavior,
   violent
American Academy of Child and
   Adolescent Psychiatry, 10, 66
American Family Association, 37
American Prospect (magazine), 83
American Psychological Association, 6–7
   Commission on Violence and Youth
      (1994), 15
American Viewpoint, 67
Ang, Ien, 15
*Assessment of the Television Industry's Use
   of V-Chip Ratings* (Kunkel et al.), 23

"Bad Boyz" (song), 60
Barrow, Shyne, 60
Basketball Diaries, The (film), 8, 79
Bauer, Gary, 76
behavior, violent
   fantasy violence causes, is "the big
      lie," 38
   is part of human nature, 54–55
   and media violence, 85
      causation vs. correlation between,
         6–7
   non-media influences on, 12, 71
Bennett, Bill, 61
Blackthorne, Alan, 27
Bonnie and Clyde (film), 41–42
Bourdieu, Pierre, 31, 32
Bozell, Brent, 14
Brandon, Teena, 25
Brownbeck, Sam, 84
Buckingham, David, 34
Butler, Robert W., 40

Campus Alliance to End Gun Violence,
   62
Carmack, John, 46, 47
Case for Television Violence, The (Fowles),
   7

censorship
   dangers of, 84–85
   early battles over, 75
   of early movies, 41
   problem of media violence does not
      justify, 82–85
Center for Media and Public Affairs, 28
Centerwall, Brandon, 71
Chadwick, Frank, 49
*Channeling Violence: The Economic Market
   for Violent Television Programming*
   (Hamilton), 19, 26
Cheney, Lynne, 84, 85
children
   are more affected by media violence,
      72–73
   average TV viewing time of, 10
   effects of media violence on
      are measurable and long-lasting, 11
      research is inconclusive, 13–17
Child's Play 3 (film), 72
Clinton, Bill, 75
Clockwork Orange, A (film), 75
Cochran, Johnnie, 59
Colorito, Rita, 24
Columbine High School shooting, 6, 40,
   45, 69, 83
   debate following, 71
Combs, Sean "Puffy," 58–59
Comics Code Authority, 56
Computer Gaming World (magazine), 52
Comstock, Anthony, 83
Condon, Charlie, 77
Conrad, Kent, 83
Constitution, U.S.
   First Amendment, 61, 84
   Second Amendment, 61
Costikyan, Greg, 49
Court TV, 27
crime
   as top category of TV news, 28
   among youth is falling as music sales
      are rising, 67
Cutler, Maggie, 13

Daikatana (video game), 46
Dateline (TV news magazine), 25, 27
*Defining Visions: Television and the
   American Experience Since 1945*
   (Watson), 8
De Luca, Mike, 71

demographics
  targeted, by television, 19
  of video game users, 51
Disney, 70, 85
Distinctions (Bourdieu), 32
Dixie Chicks, 68
Do It for the Kids!, 61
Dole, Bob, 75
Doom (video game), 45, 46

Earle, Steve, 68
Easterbrook, Gregg, 69
Easy Rider (film), 75
8MM (film), 73
Eminem, 79
entertainment industry
  censorship by, 85
  defenses of television violence used by,
    19–20
  lawsuits against, 80–81
  markets violent media to children,
    77–81
  needed reforms of, 23, 76
Eraser (film), 71
Eron, Leonard, 72

Farkas, Steve, 35
Federal Trade Commission, 77, 82.
  recommendations for recording
    industry, 65–66
48 Hours (TV news magazine), 25, 27
Fowles, Jib, 7, 30

Garbarino, James, 14
Garin-Hart Research, 67
Gerbner, George, 28
Goodbye Lover (film), 74
Gore, Al, 59, 75, 82
Gore, Tipper, 59
Grana, Sheryl, 26, 27, 29
Great Train Robbery, The (film), 41
Grossman, David, 46, 54
gun control groups
  and criticism of gangsta rap, 60–62
guns
  glamorization of, in rap music is a
    serious problem, 58–62

Hamilton, James B., 18, 26, 27
Handgun Control, Inc., 61
Harper's (magazine), 9
Harris, Eric, 7, 43, 45, 88
Hatch, Orrin, 14
Hattemer, Barbara, 36
Hebdige, Dick, 35
Heston, Charlton, 59, 60
Hollings, Fritz, 85
Holmberg, Carl, 28
Howe, Julia Ward, 83

Hwa, Nancy, 61

Jipping, Thomas L., 8

Kaminer, Wendy, 82
Keegan, Paul, 46
Klebold, Dylan, 7, 43, 45, 88
Kolbert, Elizabeth, 36
Kunkel, Dale, 23

Leo, John, 8
Lieberman, Carole, 37
Lieberman, Joseph, 15, 82, 84, 85
Los Angeles Times (newspaper), 69
*Lost Boys: Why Our Sons Turn Violent and
  How We Can Save Them* (Garbarino),
  14
Lott, John, Jr., 73
Lott, Trent, 83
Lucas, George, 42

Males, Mike, 9
Manson, Marilyn, 8
*Marketing Violent Entertainment to
  Children* (Federal Trade Commission),
  77
mass media
  as derogatory term, 32–33
Masta Ace, 62
Matrix, The (film), 40
Maxim (magazine), 51
McCain, John, 15, 83
media violence
  effects of, on children, 11
    is harmful, 10–12
  makes people more violent, 69–76
  problem does not justify censorship,
    82–85
  research on effects of, is inconclusive,
    13–17, 85
Mighty Joe Young (film), 70–71
Moriarty, Brian, 52, 53
Mortal Kombat (video game), 46
movies
  early, violence in, 41
  glamorize guns, 73–74
  ratings of
    studios control, 74–75
    and youth marketing, 78
  rise of graphic violence in, 41–42
  violence in, is a serious problem,
    40–43
  violent, profitability of, 74–76
Moxley, Martha, 25
Murdock, Graham, 39
Murphree, Randall, 37
music
  problem of violent themes in, is
    exaggerated, 63–68

rap
  "gangsta," 8
  glamorization of guns in, is a serious
    problem, 58–62
  recording industry
    voluntary guidelines program of,
      64–65
  sales are rising as youth violent crime
    is falling, 67

National Television Violence Study,
  1994–97, 7, 28
Natural Born Killers (film), 42, 45, 70, 73,
  74
Neufeld, Victor, 26, 28
New Yorker (magazine), 72
New Yorkers Against Gun Violence, 61
New York Post (newspaper), 60
New York Times (newspaper), 64, 73
Night Trap (video game), 46
Nordlinger, Jay, 58

O'Donnell, Rosie, 73
O.J. Simpson murder trial, 27, 28
opinion polls. *See* surveys
Orientalism (Said), 33

parents
  help for, is needed, 21–23
  should censor children's music, 67–68
Pascoe, Ted, 61
Peckinpah, Sam, 42
Pelosi, Andy, 61
Peterson, Sandy, 55, 56
Pitofsky, Robert, 85
Pollack, Sydney, 79
Porter, Edwin S., 41
Postal (video game), 51–52
Prince, Stephen, 88
Provenzo, Eugene F., Jr., 44
Pulp Fiction (film), 42, 70

Quake (video game), 46, 54
  appeal of, 50–51

Replacement Killers, The (film), 73
Rhodes, Richard, 9
Richman, Murray, 60
Rigolletto (Verdi), 67
Robinson, Thomas, 16
Romero, John, 46
Rosen, Hillary B., 63

Said, Edward, 33
Salome (Strauss), 67–68
*Scapegoat Generation: America's War on
  Adolescents, The* (Males), 9
school shootings, 6, 17
  and video games, 47

Scream (film), 69, 70
Screening Violence (Prince), 8
Seiter, Ellen, 33
Shane (film), 41
Skekel, Michael, 25, 27
Slouka, Mark, 47
Smarr, Larry, 46
Spice 1, 60
Spielberg, Steven, 45
St. Petersburg Times (newspaper), 62
Stallybrass, Peter, 34
Star Wars (film), 42
Stavitsky, Joe, 9
Stayner, Cary, 25, 26
Stevens, George, 41
Stone, Oliver, 45
surveys
  on adult attitudes toward youth, 35
  on influences on children, 67

Tarantino, Quentin, 8, 45, 80
Telecommunications Act of 1996, 8
television
  attack on violence on
    as attack on youth, 35–36
    as class issue, 31–32
    as gender issue, 36–37
    by religious right, 37–38
  average time spent watching, by
    children, 10
  demographic targeted by, 19
  news programs
    crime as major focus of, 28
    violence on, is a serious problem,
      24–29
  pervasiveness of, 7–8
  violence on
    economic incentives for, 21
    effects of viewing, 7
    industry defenses of, 19–20
    is a serious problem, 18–23
      con, 30–39
    in news programs, 24–29
    major consumers for, 20, 26
    during prime time, 71
Time-Warner, 70, 85
"Trigga Gots No Heart" (song), 60
Turner, Ted, 31
20/20 (TV news magazine), 25
Twitchell, James, 36

USA Today (newspaper), 71

Valenti, Jack, 79
Vargas, Elizabeth, 25
V-Chip, 22, 76
video games
  benefits of, 55
  demographics of, 51

effects of
  limited research has been done on,
    11
  violence in, is a serious problem,
    44–48
    con, 49–58
Video Kids: Making Sense of Nintendo
  (Provenzo), 44

Washington Post (newspaper), 69
Watching Dallas: Soap Opera and the

Melodramatic Imagination (Ang), 15
Watson, Mary Ann, 8
White, Allon, 34
Wild Bunch, The (film), 42
Wildmon, Donald, 37
Willard, Frances, 83
Williams, Raymond, 32
Winick and Winick study, 15, 16

Zirinsky, Susan, 25–27